TO THE PAST

Strategies for Teaching American History in Grades 5–12

JOAN BRODSKY SCHUR

Foreword by James A. Percoco

Stenhouse Publishers
Portland, Maine

Stenhouse Publishers
www.stenhouse.com

Library of Congress Cataloging-in-Publication Data

Credits:
Page 30: John Adams diary 19, 16 December 1772 - 18 December 1773 [electronic edition]. Adams Family Papers: An Electronic Archive. Massachusetts Historical Society. http://www.masshist.org/digitaladams/. Image reprinted by permission of the Massachusetts Historical Society.

Page 184: "To Colored Men! Freedom, Protection, Pay, and a Call to Military Duty!" Recruiting poster in the U. S. National Archives and Records Administration Records of the Adjutant General's Office, Record Group 94. Image courtesy of the U. S. National Archives and Records Administration website. www.archives.gov/education/lessons/black-civil-war.

Page 186: "Latest News from Washington! The rebels swarming the Potomac!" Poster owned by the New-York Historical Society. Image reprinted by permission.

Pages 222 and 224: "Photo Analysis Worksheet" and "Cartoon Analysis Worksheet" courtesy of the U. S. National Archives and Records Administration Teaching with Documents website. www.archives.gov/education/lessons/.

Schur, Joan Brodsky.
   Eyewitness to the past : strategies for teaching American history in grades 5-12 / Joan Brodsky Schur ; foreword by James A. Percoco.
      p. cm.
   Includes bibliographical references.
   ISBN-13: 978-1-57110-497-7 (pbk. : alk. paper)
   ISBN-10: 1-57110-497-6 (pbk. : alk. paper)
   1. United States--History--Study and teaching (Secondary) 2. United States--History--Study and teaching (Secondary)--Activity programs. 3. Historiography--Study and teaching (Secondary)--United States. 4. United States--Historiography. I. Title.

E175.8.S37 2007
973.071--dc22
                                             2006035224

Cover and interior design by Designboy Creative Group

Manufactured in the United States of America on acid-free paper
13 12 11 10 09 08 07   9 8 7 6 5 4 3 2

For my parents,
Samuel Brodsky and Margery Bach Brodsky,
who always make me feel proud to be a teacher.

Contents

Foreword

On a blustery March day in 1832, along the banks of the Sangamon River, a lanky twenty-three-year-old politician put forth his hopes and ambitions for himself and the frontier town as he tacked up broadside after broadside announcing his candidacy for office. The young Abraham Lincoln addressed the question of education in his announcement arguing it "the most important subject which we as a people can be engaged in." One hundred and seventy-four years later, as we approach the bicentennial of the birth of the greatest leader developed by democracy, savvy New York City history teacher Joan Brodsky Schur would well agree with Mr. Lincoln.

In *Eyewitness to the Past* Schur examines and explains six multifaceted eyewitness strategies in her approach to teaching United States history. Through her methods, she shows students that learning can be fun and lead you to places you may never have imagined. Schur presents in six easy-to-read and singularly different chapters a way to not only instill historical and critical thinking skills in students, but also life skills. They are all here—reading, writing, team building, empathy construction, and plain old-fashioned good civic behavior. Her approaches are clever, well balanced, and reflect a sense of time-honored instructional strategies while at the same time immersing students in history. Good history teachers know that diaries from the past provide a unique window to distant times. In Chapter 1, not only do her students read historical diaries, they take on a historical persona, which permits them to see, feel, and touch the past in an appreciable way, grasping the importance of historical empathy. Chapter 2 cleverly weaves the use of historical travel narratives into the teacher's tool kit. I particularly liked Schur's detective-like sleuthing at flea markets to find old postcards to help her students visualize both time *and* place. In Chapter 3 students explore how people communicated to each other in a world before blogs, instant messaging, and email; they wrote letters the old-fashioned way and so, too, do Schur's students. If you want to know how to pull off the ultimate group newspaper project, then Chapter 4 tells you how it can be done. Is persuasive writing part of your action plan for students? Chapter

5 provides tips not only for how to write a persuasive political speech, but how to get elected in the tumultuous process, while reliving the days of Andrew Jackson, Daniel Webster, and Henry Clay among others—with all the machinations and raucousness of early American politics, including banners, buntings, slogans, and songs. In Chapter 6 students study and create their own scrapbook across time, learning that this kind of personal archive project tells us not only about the person's life, but also about the time period in which he or she lived. In each of the strategies presented, Schur shows "teachers how they can make the study of history exciting by placing students in the shoes of ordinary people who, like we do now, lived in a state of suspense through tense times."

The activities and strategies presented here do not exist in a vacuum separated from the history we are making. Schur helps students to see connections between the past and present, be it with political, military, or social history providing not only a sense of immediacy but relevancy as well.

In today's climate of high stakes testing and state-mandated standards, Schur provides a much-needed breath of fresh air. She is not faint of heart and is a teacher's teacher. She knows that believing in her students is the ultimate key to her success. Experienced teachers understand the power in believing in our students, and those new to the profession can glean much from her sage advice. A life-long learner herself, Schur knows the wisdom and value of learning from her students.

In *Eyewitness to the Past* you will find not only an array of productive, useful, and teacher-friendly strategies, but you will find as well solid suggestions as to how to assess and evaluate student work, complete with matching rubrics to help you help your history students become successful learners. If you are looking for alternate strategies to move you beyond the textbook, then you will find comfort and practicality in Schur's examples. Additionally, Schur's book is loaded with tips on how to use such Internet resources as ProQuest as both a research tool for investigating historical newspaper accounts and as a model for historical writing activities.

Tapping into best practices and history's habits of the mind helps her students to recognize that in history there is no such thing as monocausality— a singular and simplistic reason for events to unfold the way they did. Her lessons provide students a way to understand and appreciate the complexity of history. In Schur's history laboratory, students look at all sides of an issue, weigh and evaluate evidence, and then offer hypotheses while being creative in the process. Like practicing historians, Schur's students conclude that there is no such thing as a definitive answer, but rather, an interpretation, which is an important acquired skill so necessary in a free, ever-evolving democratic society. Historians at their best are critical thinkers weighing and evaluating evidence that they uncover, making decisions based on the skills of their craft. In a complex society, it is vital that our young people recognize the power of such skills as they construct a history for their generation based on the groundwork laid by generations who have trod before them.

In an 1852 speech, Abraham Lincoln argued, "History is philosophy teaching by example." In *Eyewitness to the Past* you will clearly see how the ideas purported by Lincoln in the middle of the nineteenth century retain their dynamism and relevancy at the beginning of the twenty-first century in the hands of Joan Brodsky Schur.

James A. Percoco

Acknowledgments

All of the people I wish to thank value what it means to be a teacher. Teachers need as much support as they can get, or at least I know I do, because we are too little valued by society at large. I have been a teacher for more than thirty years, but I could not have sustained a happy and productive life in the classroom without the encouragement of family, friends, colleagues, and a variety of institutions whose purpose it is to reach out to teachers. Teaching is hard work, but it is also terrific fun. The emotional and intellectual rewards of working with adolescents give as much meaning to my life today as when I started out.

This book could not have been written without my students at the Village Community School whose work appears in these pages. They are forever willing to follow my game plan, take risks with me, and let me know what does not work, as well as what does. No creative idea of mine can come to fruition without their steadfast efforts. For this I am deeply indebted to them. The class of 2005–2006, as well as students from previous years, gave me permission to publish their work. They know that I have changed their names so that I can discuss their work with complete honesty.

Students like those I teach do not exist in a vacuum. By the time they have reached the eighth grade, when I teach them American history, they have had the benefit of many gifted teachers at VCS. Over the years I learned from the consummate and inspiring teachers who taught many of my students before I did, including Sari Grossman, Jennifer Trano, and Nancy Beal Mostow. My colleagues in what we call the Upper School have all contributed to the teacher I have become. Thanks to Ron Ziff for his undying belief in the value of field trips; to Nova Gutierrez, who has stretched me to think in new ways; to Laura Shearer for the comfort of her friendship and the poetry of her teaching. I also want to thank many former colleagues. Dan Schuchat read the original proposal for this book and gave the publisher invaluable advice on it. As a board member of the National Council for the Social Studies, former colleague Syd Golston's passionate dedication to our field keeps me, as well as educators across the country, inspired. Finally, Andy Robinson and I shared the kind of teaching partnership I hope every teacher can experience at least once in a lifetime.

Just as students do not learn in a vacuum, neither do teachers. Eve K. Kleger, Director of the Village Community School, has enabled me to explore new directions in my career, including the writing of this book. For this I am most grateful. Assistant Director Denise Frazier has provided me with her expert guidance in my new role as Social Studies Coordinator, in which capacity I am also grateful for the support of Melissa Gordon, school psychologist, and Jessica Spielberger, Director of the Upper School. There are also many former administrators who nurtured my work when they were at the Village Community School. The vision of Sheila E. Sadler, founding Director, continues to nourish all of us who worked with her. Janie Lou Hirsch, current Director of the Westland School in Los Angeles, kept me laughing while teaching me everything I needed to know about adolescents. Jeff W. Wallis encouraged me to take risks. Arthur Whitman never failed to show his appreciation for the hard work and talent of the teachers under his caring wing. I would also like to thank all my current colleagues from whom I continue to learn and with whom it is my great privilege to work.

The value of teaching with documents is an important theme throughout this book. I first explored the potential of using primary sources in the 1970s while working at the City & Country School in New York City. Their library collection is designed to facilitate teaching with documents, and my experiences there set me on the path to becoming the teacher I am now. In 1991 I attended the Primarily Teaching workshop at the National Archives, a program that has changed the lives of many teachers, including mine. No word of thanks would be complete without expressing my gratitude to Wynell Schamel for her inspiration then as well as for her continuing support. It was in 1998 that Lee Ann Potter took me into the digital age by inviting me to work with a group of remarkable educators to write lesson plans for the National Archives Digital Classroom website. It was a gift and a turning point in my career to work under her dynamic leadership. I am also extremely thankful for the wisdom of her feedback on the original proposal for this book. Kim Barbieri, Education Specialist at the Dwight D. Eisenhower Presidential Library, has been a cheerleader and helpmate over many years. Thomas Gray, an expert on teaching with documents, has extended his help to me at the drop of a hat on numerous occasions.

A number of the ideas I share in this book first appeared in articles I wrote for *Social Education*, where Michael Simpson's encouragement as well as insight into the needs of teachers were critical to their success. The ideas for other teaching strategies were first hatched while I was writing lesson plans for PBS under the keen guidance of Mary Kadera and Tim Walker. I also want to thank Mary for the opportunity to serve on the TeacherSource Advisory Group from 2002–2004. From her visionary thinking I learned how important it is to work on teams and to look ahead to the future of technology in education. I also want to thank Anne Harrington of WETA, the PBS station in Washington, D.C., who gave me the golden opportunity to write lesson plans for many documentaries by Ken Burns.

Writing the proposal for this book made me realize how very much I learned from my former editor at Lucent Books, Lauri Friedman. James A. Percoco's marvelous books on teaching American history inspired me to take the plunge and write my own. Danny Miller's original enthusiasm for this project is what set it in motion. A thanks to Erin Whitehead for her scrupulous and thoughtful work on the manuscript. Most of all I wish to thank Bill Varner at Stenhouse Publishers who spent many months patiently answering my many questions. His wise and consummate judgment helped the book take shape in many important ways.

The encouragement, support, and patience of many friends saw me through a long and hard year of writing. Among them are my sister and dearest friend, Alice Brodsky Forcier; Susan Gill, whose steadfast friendship I treasure; Christine Eickelman, who knows me as well as I know myself; Pamela Berge, with whom I shared much book talk throughout the year; and Sally Downs, whose hospitality I always value. Without the joyous encouragement of Irv and Sue Sarnoff I might never have written this book at all.

My daughter, Sarah Brodsky Schur, has always valued the importance of what I do in life, and her appreciation has meant a great deal to me over the years. I also want to thank the newcomer in our family, our little dog Phoebe, who sat patiently on the orange chair while I typed away.

To my husband, Edwin M. Schur, I owe the most thanks. He has appreciated how much teaching means to me over three decades. He led the way in showing me that teachers can develop a wide-ranging professional life beyond their own classrooms. With the rigor of a lawyer and a professor and the gentleness of a helpmate, Ed taught me how to write, sentence by sentence, in the early years of our marriage. Thank you, Ed.

Chapter One

History from the Eyewitness Viewpoint

When I first started teaching, I thought it would be easy to impart my enthusiasm for history to my students. I imagined that if I shared the facts and stories that fascinated me, my audience would naturally be fascinated, too. But just because I love New York City where I grew up does not mean that I can convince you that you should love it. Soon enough I realized that conveying information, no matter how interesting to me, was not sufficient to engage my students. I had to think about the *processes* through which students acquired information so that history became meaningful to them.

First I had to figure out why most students find history boring rather than exciting. Since we are living through times that will become history, perhaps our own experiences hold the key. During recent events like the war in Iraq or the last presidential election, we all lived in a state of tension and suspense. We listened eagerly and anxiously to friends, family members, colleagues, and television commentators. We read books, editorials, and blogs written by people who may have agreed or disagreed with us, changed our way of thinking, or infuriated us. Changes in immigration policy or health insurance were not abstract matters, but directly affected many of us and those we care about. As teachers we need to ask ourselves, Why will these same events as recounted in textbooks bore students a decade from now? The answer in part is that the outcome of the events will be known, the controversies they generated will be omitted from textbooks, and their effects on ordinary people will be overlooked.

In *Eyewitness to the Past* I share a variety of classroom strategies based on my years of teaching eighth-grade American history as well as teaching English. My goal is to show teachers how they can make the study of history exciting by placing students in the shoes of ordinary people who, like we do now, lived in a state of suspense through tense times. Ordinary people in times past cared passionately about what the future would hold because they had a personal stake in what happened next. In order for students to make an imaginative leap into the lives of generations long gone, students need to hear the voices of people as witnessed in their letters, diaries, daily newspapers, speeches, and autobiographies. This approach emphasizes the fact that common citizens affected the course of events, just as average people today make an impact on history. And it is crucial to a true understanding of history that students not just listen to the winning side. Students need to hear from the Tories as well as from the Rebels, the slave owners as well as the abolitionists, the men and even women who opposed female suffrage and not just the suffragists. In the activities described in this book, the documents left to us, representing multiple views, become models for student writing and oral argument. With the help of these models, students imaginatively live through past events without "knowing" what will happen next or how it will affect their imagined lives.

I call the activities described in this book *eyewitness strategies* because students relive historic events as if they were there. In this approach, students rely on the their textbooks, supplemented by primary source documents, to see events through the prism of an imagined persona (or sometimes a group of people) with a particular viewpoint. Once invested in a point of view, students hold a personal stake in what will happen next. The classroom comes alive because debates naturally arise from a situation in which people hold different or opposing viewpoints.

To understand what mattered to people living in a different era, students need to be familiar with the details of their daily lives—what they wore, what their homes looked like, what expectations governed their social interactions. To experience the excitement of history, students must also be able to envision it. It is important for students to see the past as it was depicted in advertisements, portraits, photographs, and film when available. Thus each eyewitness strategy incorporates the use of both written and visual primary source documents. Visits to museums and historic homes take on new meaning when they hold a place in students' imaginations as well. Student-produced artwork (whether generated by hand or computer) is an important aspect of each strategy because it helps students visualize the past.

The Six Eyewitness Strategies

This book is organized into six eyewitness strategies. Each chapter covers one strategy and describes a sequence of activities that can be adapted to accommodate different content. Each strategy focuses on one type of written primary source document: diaries, travelogues, letters, newspapers, election speeches, and scrapbooks. Students study the properties of that genre and its use to historians in understanding the past before they write in that genre themselves. With each strategy, the class ends up generating work from a variety of viewpoints, thus creating a more complex appreciation for the texture of American life. I illustrate how I developed each strategy in the classroom by discussing a particular application of the strategy to one time period in U.S. history, and show how it can be easily adapted to teach other events and eras as well. Because each strategy generates controversy and debate, I also suggest ways to conclude each unit with role-plays and simulations. Engaging their minds, imaginations, and multiple intelligences ensures that all students will find at least one route through which history becomes meaningful. Samples of student work and rubrics for assessment accompany each chapter.

My goal is to provide clear instructions so that teachers can easily implement and adapt each eyewitness strategy. But in addition, each chapter is packed full with inventive teaching ideas for analyzing documents and understanding point of view that can stand on their own as wonderful activities in the classroom.

Overview of the Six Eyewitness Strategies

Diaries: Writing from Opposing Viewpoints

In this chapter, students read examples of historical diaries and then create a persona and write a diary of their own. They keep their diaries while they "live through" a set of events as they "unfold" in their textbooks. The class is divided into different viewpoints on the same events (Rebels and Tories, for example). Students maintain these viewpoints as they write their diaries and discuss events in class. They create covers for their diaries that depict their homes or crafts.

Travelogues: Eyewitness Perspectives on a Growing Nation

Historians have an incredible array of travelogues written by those who journeyed across America at various times in our history. After reading samples from travelogues and related chapters in textbooks, students imagine themselves in the role of a traveler with a particular purpose: explorer, land speculator, immigrant, or conservationist, for example. Thus they describe what they see from a particular perspective while gaining an appreciation for America during a particular time period. In addition to writing, students create sketches and artwork of what they see along the way.

Letters: Arguing the Past in Written Correspondence

After reading examples of historical letters, students are put into pairs of correspondents. The students in each role-playing pair write a series of letters to one another while holding different perspectives on the issues they are learning about from their textbooks. Correspondents might be stationed on the home front and battlefront during a war or be supporters of opposing presidential candidates. Enclosures in their letters include family photographs or sketches and a variety of keepsakes such as news clippings about important events of the time.

Newspapers: Conflicting Accounts of the Same Events

With an ever-increasing number of documents now available online, students can easily access examples of news articles written at various times in our history and expressing different viewpoints. After studying how language can slant our take on events, teams of students are assigned to write their own newspapers that represent partisan perspectives of key events of the day such as a Civil War battle or controversial trial. Students also generate advertisements and cartoons that put events in sociological as well as historical perspective.

Election Speeches: Advocating for Your Candidate

Campaigning and speechifying have been integral parts of the democratic process since our nation's founding. This eyewitness strategy is set during a presidential election year and focuses on the rhetoric of speeches. Students are divided into teams, each in support of one presidential candidate. Each student writes a speech in favor of one aspect of his or her candidate's platform and presents the speech in a formal debate. Students also generate cartoons, slogans, posters, and, for modern campaigns, radio and television advertisements.

Scrapbooks: Documenting the Past Across Time

Scrapbooks are a means to preserve and reflect on how historic events play a role in personal or family histories. They demonstrate how politics, social trends, and technology affect our private and professional lives. In this activity students work alone or in family groups to create a collection of memorabilia that demonstrates the impact history makes on individuals and their families.

Adapting and Sequencing the Eyewitness Strategies

When I adapt one of these strategies, I go to the textbook first. Despite their touted differences (this one highlights geography, another primary sources or graphic organizers, and so forth), American history textbooks all tell much the same story in much the same sequence. Titles of chapters may vary, but content remains fairly constant over the long haul. If I am teaching about the social and technological changes of the 1920s with an emphasis on the women's rights movement, I might assign a scrapbook. Grandma's generation would be preflapper and pre-automobile. Mother's generation (after women get the vote) would feel the full effects of the Jazz Age. If I am teaching the 1930s, I might choose to cover it in a travelogue since I want students to see how different regions of the country are being affected by the Great Depression. A set of historical events, such as those leading up to the Revolution or Civil War, lends itself to a diary or letter exchange sequence.

Here is a possible sequence to cover the first half of a typical U.S. history textbook:

- Personal diaries during events leading to the Revolution
- Election debate of 1800: Adams versus Jefferson
- Travelogue describing life in America in the early 1830s
- Letter exchange set in the 1850s with a focus on events leading to the Civil War
- Conflicting news accounts of a Civil War battle
- Scrapbook of life during Reconstruction

In such a sequence students would be learning about America's first one hundred years as a nation, encompassing the life spans of two to three generations. Thus it is not too hard for a student to imagine that the character he or she develops in the Revolutionary War diary then traveled around America in the 1820s, perhaps settling out West and voting for Andrew Jackson in 1832 at age seventy. Perhaps that individual's offspring lived through events leading to the Civil War and into Reconstruction. We truly are a young country, after all! While students are not expected to develop a family saga throughout the sequence of eyewitness strategies, they should be encouraged to imagine the characters they create living through time. There was not, after all, a generation that was born in 1776 and dropped dead all at once in 1787 when the Constitution was ratified. Americans living in the Roaring Twenties were not all born in 1920 only to die with the stock market crash in 1929. Indeed, some people living in the 1920s fought in the Civil War, while others would live into the 1980s, and so forth.

Another sequence for using the eyewitness strategies for the second half of U.S. history might look like this:

- Scrapbooks of immigrants arriving during the Great Migration of 1880 to 1925

- Travelogues of Americans during the Great Depression
- Letter exchanges between individuals on the battlefront and home front during World War II
- Diaries during the Cold War era
- Conflicting news accounts of the Vietnam War and the Tet Offensive
- Election debate between Jimmy Carter and Ronald Reagan in 1980

Here again we can easily imagine an overall story of two or three generations. A young child arrives in America with his or her immigrant parents, lives through the Great Depression and World War II, and raises children who fight in and/or protest the war in Vietnam.

Because this second sequence takes place during and after the advent of radio, film, and television, students can access primary sources created with these new technologies. It is not difficult to find famous speeches online and hear their original audio recordings, for example. Students can also interview people in their own communities who lived through these events. Finally, students can make use of twenty-first century technologies to create their own documents. Rather than produce printed newspapers, they can create conflicting radio accounts of the same events or videotape their election debates and broadcast them on video or DVD. At the same time, students can study the effects of new media on the political process.

The Role of the Textbook

The textbook is a fact of life in schools across the country. It thus becomes tempting to make the study of history synonymous with learning only what is in the text, boring or not. Rather than give in to this predicament, I view the textbook as both a tool and a challenge. It is a useful one-stop source of information, but how can I motivate students to feel they are living participants in history, despite the monotonous voice of the text?

The strategies that are developed in this book ensure that students learn and review events covered in the text. Because students have to personalize information from their textbook as they imaginatively incorporate it into assignments, they retain information and learn it in depth. Because the class explores events from multiple viewpoints, students are able to replace a voiceless and presumably objective viewpoint with multiple and sometimes conflicting interpretations. This leads students to a better understanding of how historians construct a story of the past.

Critical Thinking Skills

Although I distribute textbooks to my students every year, I want them to apply their critical thinking skills to the information presented in the text right away. Thus, before I assign any reading in the text, I read to the class Howard Zinn's account of Columbus from *A People's History of the United States* (1980). Zinn draws on primary source documents to present the horrifying history of what happened to the Arawak Indians in the wake of Columbus's landing on the island of Hispaniola. He then claims, "When we read the history books given to children in the United States, it all starts with heroic adventure—there is no bloodshed—and Columbus Day is a celebration" (7). I ask students whether they think Zinn's accusation, written more than twenty-five years ago, still stands. When they open their textbooks they discover, quite sadly, that Zinn is still essentially correct. We compare Zinn's account of Columbus's exploration to the one presented in their textbook point for point. I ask students, Is any piece of information in one account directly contradicted in the other? What gets left out of each version? How do omissions slant our perspective? What else would you want to know to determine the truth? Where would you find out? At what age should students be presented with "the whole truth," especially if it is upsetting? Is it ever possible to accomplish telling the whole story in a textbook? What is the purpose of a textbook? Should it attempt to instill national pride? Why and why not? These are some of the questions that make students think and that generate good debate because they are open-ended.

Deconstructing the Text

Another effective way to help students deconstruct the text is to ask them to investigate how textbooks get written and approved for state adoption, especially in the case of states like California and Texas, which have enormous influence on the textbook industry because of their purchasing power and review process. My students were upset to discover that the

Texas board of education was able to get a publishing company to revise its statement on global warming, for example, so that it would be adoptable by the lucrative Texas market. The controversy about teaching evolution surely did not end with the Scopes Trial in 1925. As our year progresses, I ask my students if they think their textbook accurately conveys the importance that religion played throughout American history.

Who should decide what students read? This is the issue I let students grapple with and debate among themselves. But even when students answer, "Historians," I do not let them assume the matter is so simple. I assign students to read a *New York Times* article written by Alexander Stille (2002). In it John Mack Faragher, a history professor at Yale University, is quoted as saying,

> *There was no women's history until there was a women's movement, there was no African-American history before there was a civil rights movement. Historical practice is very much determined by the things that people are concerned about. History is ultimately a moral art, and it is about values. It is not merely about the collection of facts. It is about the way we put those facts together and the meaning we give them. (A1)*

When I assign readings in our textbook they remember this statement. The facts are there in the text, presented in such a way that appears neutral, but multiple interpretations of them are possible. As students cull their text for facts to use in the eyewitness documents they create, they need to think about what those facts *signify* within a given context. Information in the textbook becomes meaningful and therefore easier to remember.

Historiography

I encourage my students to scrutinize their textbooks as historiography, not just history. By comparing what James M. McPherson writes about Reconstruction in the textbook *The American Journey* (Appleby, Brinkley, and McPherson 2003) to a version I read in school in the early 1960s, students can begin to understand how and why interpretations change. The pre-civil rights text that I grew up with was strictly out of *Gone With the*

Wind—it described carpetbaggers descending like vultures on the South to enrich themselves and oppress the vanquished white population by ensuring that unqualified African Americans (mere lackeys of the carpetbaggers) would be elected to office. This depiction of the Reconstruction era was used to justify the maintenance of segregation until historians like Kenneth Stampp wrote revisionist works about the period in the 1960s, such as *The Era of Reconstruction, 1865–1877* (1965).

Another tack is to ask students to evaluate the way their textbook presents the end of World War II. Growing up in the fifties and early sixties, I took many years to fully comprehend the true role the Soviet Union played in defeating Hitler and the debt we owed to the Russians. During the Cold War years this was not something the powers-that-be emphasized in U.S. textbooks.

It is also fun to ask students to reverse national perspectives by writing a textbook chapter on the Mexican War of 1846 to 1848 from a Mexican perspective or by writing a Canadian version of the French and Indian War. One year my students came to class with their textbook notes on the Mexican War in hand. I surprised them when I insisted that we discuss events of the war as if we were Mexicans living in Mexico, reversing the use of the pronouns *we* and *they*. Following this I invited a fellow teacher at my school to come to talk to us about her Chicano family's long history in South Texas.

Students can apply their new understanding of the complexities of textbook perspectives to current issues as well. How would students objectively summarize the U.S. invasion of Iraq in 2003 were they writing a textbook today? What happens to their use of language when they try to present a neutral tone? These activities use the text while demanding that students question its authority through critical thinking skills.

What If?

Another means of getting students to use the text while enabling them to think outside the box is to make use of the "What If?" approach to history. When we look back on a sequence of historical events, they seem to have unfolded inevitably. But they need not have happened that way. To be engaged in those events imaginatively from an eyewitness perspective, students must feel they could have made a difference in how events turned out. If we want students to be active citizens today, if we want them to feel empowered to make wise decisions that will affect future generations, we need to teach them to analyze the consequences of decisions past. This is where the "What If?" approach to history can be fun and useful. According to Robert Cowley (2003),

> *Counterfactual history may be the history of what didn't happen, a shadow universe, but it casts a reflective light on what did. Why did certain events (and the trends and trajectories that grew out of them) dominate, and not others? At what point did possibilities become impossibilities? Why did America develop in the way that it did when it could easily have followed other directions? Critics attack such speculations as being mere entertainment, mind games lacking in intellectual rigor or seriousness. I would maintain that they can be entertaining and educational at the same time. (xiii)*

What if America had lost the Revolutionary War? What if the South had won the Civil War? What if the Watergate scandal had never been uncovered? By discussing what did not happen, students can begin to understand the grave consequences of what *did*. Students also feel more at liberty to enter history not only through their intellects, but also through their imaginations—a liberty we regularly extend to filmmakers and writers but rarely to students.

The Role of Primary Source Documents

Reading primary sources exposes students to the multiple voices and viewpoints we want them to use to make the past come alive. Here lies the challenge of taking the raw stuff of history and making sense of it for ourselves. Learning to teach with primary sources did not come easily to me for the simple reason that I was never taught this way as a student myself. Using primary sources is a process I learned while teaching at the City & Country School in New York City. The school's commitment to teaching with primary sources dates back to its founding in 1914, so by the time I joined the faculty in the 1970s, its library had an incomparable collection of books for teaching American history. The catalog included autobiographies, collected letters, and travel journals. In 1991 I participated in Primarily Teaching, the teacher-training workshop still offered by the National Archives. There, under the expert guidance of archivists and their education staff, I researched a topic of interest to me—antislavery petitions to Congress in the 1830s—through access to the actual documents. While teaching eighth grade American history and English at the Village Community School for the past twenty-five years I have benefited immeasurably from the ongoing support of the school to keep learning and exploring ways to make history come alive through documents.

It is a positive development that some states, including New York, now mandate teaching with primary sources. For students enrolled in Advanced Placement courses, documents take center stage. Yet, it is quite disappointing to see the workbooks that are now put out to help students practice using primary sources. They are filled with short, out-of-context exercises in which students read a portion of text (a primary source) and answer questions about it—just like they do with their textbook! As Keith C. Barton and Linda Levstik (2004) report in *Teaching History for the Common Good*,

> *This is surely the form of inquiry without its substance, a tool without all its parts, faith without works. Where is the felt difficulty, the perplexity, confusion, or doubt in this kind of activity? When the questions arise from 'reproducible student pages' rather than from students' own concerns about the past, then the activity does not involve inquiry in any meaningful sense— it simply involves the analysis of documents.(199)*

There certainly are many collections of primary source documents for teachers to use, many issued by the textbook companies themselves. But to my mind, too many of them end up presenting a view of America's past that is as simplistic as the textbook's. This is because they often only present the voices of the winning side—the politically correct view. Left out are those who argued that slavery was a blessing for the African, that workers had no rights relative to their employers, and that the Chinese should not be eligible for U.S. citizenship. We lose sight of the epic proportions of the struggle for justice when the proponents of oppression are missing from the story.

Take for example the internment of Japanese Americans during World War II. This shameful part of our history is no longer hidden under the rug. Documents relating to it are included in anthologies, but editors typically choose a narrative from someone who was interned. It is much more difficult to find the voices of those supporting this policy—and most Americans either claimed not to know about it or agreed that internment was a necessary safety precaution after the Japanese bombed Pearl Harbor. How then can students learn to compare the past to the present in a meaningful way if they are not exposed to both sides of a controversy as people lived through it? It seems obvious to us *now* that the way we treated Japanese American citizens was reprehensible, but during a war whose outcome is unknown, fear can trump reason. Students need to question whether the same thing is happening today after terrorists bombed the World Trade Center on September 11, 2001. Unless students hear from both sides, they lack the tools with which they can evaluate the best course of action.

In order to help students experience the past as it was lived—from multiple overlapping and conflicting viewpoints—it is worth looking for anthologies that present contemporaneous views from various perspectives. Documents in these anthologies will supplement all six eyewitness strategies. Students need to hear the full chorus of American voices, even if the sound is often not harmonious. The series I like the best is *Opposing Viewpoints in American History* from Greenhaven Press. Here we have arguments from all sides—why the Sedition Acts violate the Bill of Rights, and why they do not, why the Louisiana Purchase should be approved and why it should not. We hear from Frederick Douglass in "Blacks Should Have the Right to Vote" but also hear from the opposition in "Blacks Should Not Have the Right to Vote" by Henry Davis McHenry, a Democrat from Kentucky. In addition to this two-volume anthology, Greenhaven puts out many single-volume editions that focus on opposing viewpoints throughout specific eras in American history, such as the American Revolution and the Vietnam War. Teachers also can find digitized primary sources on the Web such as those at the National Archives and Library of Congress, among others.

In the six eyewitnesses strategies I present, the uses of primary sources are many. First and foremost in each chapter I focus on one *type* of document, such as letters, diaries, speeches, news articles, and so on. I model ways in which students can learn to analyze each type of document much as a historian would. Because students also generate their own documents in each of the primary source categories, they have increased motivation to study the originals. Today students can use computer programs to create a variety of visual special effects to make their written documents look real, but staining them with tea is still quite a lot of fun. In addition to written documents, the eyewitness strategies incorporate the analysis and creation of visual artifacts such as illustrations, advertisements, cartoons, and so forth. Finally I suggest some documents that are valuable because of their content (e.g., the viewpoint they present). These resources are listed in the appendix and organized by chapter and category.

Documents written before the twentieth century can be daunting for students to read, with their unfamiliar words and long, convoluted sentences. My job is to make reading them as easy as possible. What I want students to understand first is the overall context of the document—who wrote it, for what purpose, and for what audience. Students will experience success if they get the general meaning first, and some of this can be gleaned by pulling out key words. If I download a document from the Web, I handwrite word definitions in the margins before photocopying it for students. I also like to read primary sources out loud. Because I know where to pause and what to emphasize as I read, their meaning is immediately more apparent to students. Asking students to circle the subject of each sentence can help. The most important thing to remember is that it is only by reading *more* and not less that students will begin to gain the confidence they need.

The Eyewitness Strategies and Adolescent Learners

I developed the methods described in this book while teaching eighth graders. The strategies can be easily adapted for middle school through high school by considering the level of the students and altering the degree to which the teacher simplifies or builds upon the suggested activities. The strategies are not appropriate for early elementary grades because they ask students to see events from multiple perspectives, a confusing concept for younger children.

The eyewitness strategies appeal to adolescents because in most of them students develop their own personas, an alter-ego "self." I give them lots of prompts to help them develop their personas, such as filling in questionnaires about their imaginary selves, while helping students to be as historically accurate as possible. By being asked to create a different self living in a different time period, students surpass their circumscribed focus on the here-and-now and extend their understanding of the world. The eyewitness strategies then become more complex as students share viewpoints and analyze multiple perspectives, their causes, and their consequences on subsequent events.

Teaching to Meet the Standards

Each eyewitness strategy is designed to accommodate a variety of historical periods described in a typical U. S. history textbook. Think of each strategy as a vessel into which you can pour the content. This makes it easy to implement a creative approach while guaranteeing to supervisors that you are covering the material mandated by your district or state.

Although there are statewide variations on what teachers are required to cover, there are also useful national guidelines. When I design a lesson, especially one for a nationally used website like PBS Online, there are several sources I go to. One is McREL (Mid-continent Research for Education and Learning), which is an online compendium of K–12 content standards and related tools for teachers designing units. Another is *Expectations of Excellence: Curriculum Standards for the Social Studies* (1994) published by the National Council for the Social Studies. It posits ten thematic strands that social studies programs should cover, including "Time, Continuity, and Change," "Science, Technology, and Society," and "Power, Authority, and Governance." Specific performance objectives are offered for each strand at the early grades, middle grades, and high school levels. Let us suppose that you want students to write opposing eyewitness newspapers (Chapter 4) of the Scopes Trial of 1925. In this activity students would be studying how scientific discoveries affect and change society, what governmental bodies mediated the dispute, and the consequences of the trial, thus covering the three thematic strands listed above.

The *National Standards for History* (1996) developed by the National Center for History in the Schools divides U.S. history into ten eras and offers standards for grades K–4 and 5–12. In addition to content guidelines, they offer five Standards in Historical Thinking. We can imagine how these historical thinking standards would be implemented if you followed the suggestions in Chapter 2, Diaries: Writing from Opposing Viewpoints. In the sequence described in Chapter 2, students live through the events of the Revolution as either Tories or Rebels. The activity enhances their ability to understand sequence (Chronological Thinking standard) because they are "living" through events in chronological order. By reading and analyzing primary sources to incorporate into their diaries students gain a better understanding of how history is constructed and written (Historical Comprehension standard). Because students are studying the Revolution from opposing viewpoints, they "consider multiple perspectives" and "challenge arguments of historical inevitability" (Historical Analysis and Interpretation standard). In order to incorporate facts into their diaries they need to do research (Historical Research Capabilities standard). At the end of an eyewitness strategy, students are ready to do higher-level thinking about events (Historical Issues-Analysis and Decision-Making standard) such as analyzing "the interests and values of the various people involved" or evaluating "the consequences of a decision." The means to achieve these last two goals are suggested at the end of each chapter and often involve a decision-making role-play.

Minimizing the Workload

Most of the eyewitness strategies discussed in this book ask students to do a significant amount of writing. As an English and social studies teacher I am well aware of the pressure this puts on educators who simply do not have the time to read and respond to everything students write. My answer to this dilemma may surprise some teachers: Assign the work anyway, then find creative ways around this inevitable problem. Our students will never learn to write if they do not write all the time.

Over the years I have adapted many strategies to keep my students writing while keeping myself sane. I always thoroughly respond to work that is being revised for the public to see, whether it will be shared in print, online, or on a bulletin board. Unless they are required to fix their mistakes, most students do not pay attention to all those red marks. So I do not waste my efforts; I want them to pay off. I usually am not the first reader who has looked for mistakes or made suggestions for improvement of the content. I often pair students or put them into writer's workshop groups to do this for one another before a draft gets to me.

This year I experimented with using the track changes feature in Microsoft Word. It is widely adopted in the business world and therefore a valuable tool for students to learn. Essentially, students email their work to me or post it electronically on our class bulletin board. I download it to my computer where I turn on the track change feature and make my comments and corrections directly on the electronic version of their papers. I email their work back to them and students then have the option to accept my changes or not and can make further revisions.

Obviously, not all student work is meant for public eyes. This means that most of the time I look for other strategies to maintain student motivation while keeping my workload manageable. English teachers are well aware of these time-saving methods. If you are lucky you may find an English teacher who is willing to teach some of the eyewitness strategies as a joint social studies and English venture. Because each of the six strategies presented in this book demands the production of a different genre of work, with varying content matter, specific rubrics can be found at the end of each chapter. These convey standards for both English skills and social studies content and concepts.

It always helps students when they are given the rubrics ahead of time so they know in advance how they will be evaluated. In each category students can earn from one to five points. A student who does not follow instructions and whose work reflects little to no mastery of English skills and social studies content receives a one. This student's work is given no credit and thus the student must redo it. A student who has followed the assignment but completed it perfunctorily or with a lack of real understanding receives a two. This work is passable but because it needs greater attention I encourage the student to hand in another draft. This student may need help using a historical document as a model for his or her own writing as well as an appreciation for how documents reflect point of view. The category for three points reflects a solid effort that squarely meets my expectations for mastery of facts and concepts. This student writes with clarity and consistency. He or she includes many factual details, synthesizes, them, and demonstrates an understanding of ideas and viewpoint. Very good work earns a four. This student has not only learned the material, but also brought it to life through the expressive use of language like that used in the time period we are studying. A student working at this level demonstrates nuanced thinking about complex issues. A student receives a five for outstanding work and original thinking. This student is often a gifted writer and avid reader who brings to the task extensive learning acquired not only in the classroom but well beyond it.

In strategizing how to maximize the effect of my feedback to students, I pay special attention to the first assignment in a series. For example, if students are writing a sequence of four letters, I want to make certain that they are on the right track as early as possible. I focus my time responding to their first letter, because if they do not understand what they are expected to do they will run into problems in subsequent letters. However, I may well not have the time to respond to each student's first letter individually. In that case, I might read out loud to the class some student work that best exemplifies what I am looking for in the assignment. Anonymously, of course, I might also read out loud an example of student work that is lacking on some score as well. For their subsequent letters I might ask some students to read aloud their work in class on a rotating basis or I might skim their letters, evaluating them based on just a few criteria each time. For example, I might say to the class, "On the next assignment I will be looking to see that you incorporate at least five facts into your letters, and that you write in complete sentences." Or I might announce, "This time I will be looking for a well-reasoned explanation of why you do or not support the tactics used in the Boston Tea Party. I will also pay special attention to your spelling." Then I read that set of letters with only those things in mind, which makes the process much quicker for me. Or I might not read several of the letters at all. Instead, I might ask students to keep their letters in a portfolio of their work and then ask them to choose the one letter they think reflects their best work for me to grade.

Conclusion

Even if you only implement one or two of the eyewitness strategies discussed in this book, you will discover that students find history as exciting as many of the most dramatic current events. Each strategy is sequenced in such a way that the past becomes both understandable and meaningful. The strategies draw on students' critical thinking skills as well as their imaginations and artistic abilities. The strategies demand that students formulate ideas and opinions and learn to express them in writing. Furthermore, the six eyewitness strategies are designed to lead to interactive debate and activities in class on an ongoing basis—they form part of a whole learning experience in which students engage with one another and not just the teacher.

If you implement several eyewitness strategies over the course of a year you will discover that students become more fluent writers and more adept at role-playing. They look forward to coming to class because they know that everyone has something different to say. Students begin to take on the excited voices of impassioned citizens who had tough choices to make, rather than the monotone voices of students answering rote questions. In developing these materials with my students over many years, my appreciation of the American past has deepened because of what they have added to our discussions. It is because of their diverse talents as thinkers, writers, and artists that these eyewitness strategies exist.

Chapter Two

I am but an ordinary Man. The Times alone have destined me
to Fame—

Diary of John Adams, 1779

Wittingly or not, diarists bequeath to historians valuable eyewitness
accounts in which they testify to their own life experiences. It is noteworthy
that we associate the very words *eyewitness* and *testify* with trials: an
eyewitness provides evidence, but not all eyewitnesses need agree on
what they saw or what it meant. Perceiving American history through
an eyewitness perspective does two useful things: it puts us back in time
experiencing events contemporaneously and it immediately takes us into
the realm of conflicting perspectives. Both of these consequences engender
excitement and debate in the classroom.

Finding primary source diaries to teach American history is not
difficult. According to Thomas Mallon (1984), "As long as there have been
Americans there have been American diaries. They were, in fact, being
written as the first boats approached the shores" (106). Many famous
people wrote diaries to enhance their reputations, knowing they would be

read by others, while some Americans became famous merely because they kept diaries. A selection covering both categories of people would include the likes of William Bradford, Jonathan Edwards, Martha Ballard, Henry David Thoreau, Louisa May Alcott, George Templeton Strong, Charlotte Forten, Charles Lindbergh, and Zelda and F. Scott Fitzgerald.

Despite their prominence as primary sources, I did not initially see the potential value of reading and writing diaries when it came to teaching the American Revolution. I felt an extra sense of responsibility about the subject matter; it was part of my patriotic duty to teach it well. Yet the events and people were not real enough in my own imagination to make them come alive for students. Washington and Jefferson seemed frozen in time, as alive as marble statues. Another difficulty was that I felt it was valid to teach only the "right" side of the story, the winning story, and we all know how it turned out. Teaching history this way is like asking students to watch an exciting basketball game *after* they know which team won, and who wants to watch a replay? We can see in our terminology for studying the era how retrospective politics come into play. The colonists who revolted against Britain's rule are alternatively called the Rebels and the Patriots, but certainly never Traitors, by which term we would know them if they had lost.

Creating a Persona

Now that I use diary writing to help students relive the Revolution from multiple perspectives, it comes alive for all of us. Similar assignments can be designed for any number of time periods in American history, such as the Civil War, the Vietnam War, and the Cold War. My goal in any case is not to assign the typical one-shot diary assignment, a creative but dead-end assignment, but rather a continuous sequence, an imaginative viewpoint through which students incorporate historical facts on an ongoing basis.

The first thing I want students to do is to imagine the persona of their diary writer and develop this fictional character. Who would these characters be? Where would they live? Students in my American history class start off the year by researching one of the thirteen colonies. This enables me to draw on the proprietary feeling each student develops about "his" or "her" colony when it comes time to study the Revolution. Too often a research project dies with a final comment or a grade, its purpose fulfilled. The colony research, however, has a second life because I ask students to take out their papers and actually make use of what they have learned. They recall why their colony was founded, how its terrain and resources affected livelihood and lifestyles, the problems that confronted the first generation of European settlers, and the consequences for its native populations. They draw on prior knowledge to imagine someone who might have lived in their colony several generations after its founding. A student who researched Pennsylvania might imagine herself to be a Quaker living in bustling Philadelphia, while a student who researched Georgia might imagine herself to be the prosperous descendant of a debtor rescued from years in an English jail by George Oglethorpe.

After students have developed their personas, I draw on another assignment I frequently make and integrate it into the diary assignment. This is a poster board display or PowerPoint presentation of a colonial craft or profession. The craft or profession assignment enables students to imagine roles they can play in their diaries. These include colonial governor, plantation owner, sea captain, school teacher, minister, printer, tavern owner, cobbler, iron monger, wig maker, silversmith, gunsmith, miller, wheelwright, and for women, midwife, housewife, sister, or widow to of any of the above. Alice Morse Earle's book *Home Life in Colonial Days* (1993) describes the arduous and artful tasks that women performed on a daily basis. After reading about any of these, students gain a new respect for what the role of a housewife entailed. Because colonists often lived and worked in the same dwelling, many women assisted men with various aspects of their trades as well. Assuming that at least one student occupies each role on my list, students recreate colonial village life in the classroom as they begin to interact with one another on that basis.

I also encourage students to imagine themselves as enslaved or free Africans, many of whom were skilled craftspeople. Poet Phillis Wheatley (1753?–1784) and mathematician and astronomer Benjamin Banneker (1731–1806) both lived through the Revolutionary period. Crispus Attucks died in the Boston Massacre. Real-life characters can provide inspiration for imagined ones. There is no reason why students cannot put themselves in the shoes of someone of a different gender or race, and I encourage them to do so. If they feel uncomfortable with this idea I tell them that novelists do this all the time and they could not write fiction otherwise. Students' ability to write historical fiction will of course be strengthened if they can simultaneously read books like Howard Fast's *April Morning* or the Colliers' *My Brother Sam is Dead*.

In order to help students share what they learned about colonial living from their crafts research, I hold a brainstorming session in which they list all the items the colonists made of wood. We compare this to a list of materials from which things are made today. The colonists had no steel, no plastic, no synthetic containers! They handcrafted everything they used, mainly out of wood. In another effort to help students appreciate how different the lives of our ancestors were from our own, a teacher at my school shows the PBS program *Colonial House* to students and finds them utterly riveted as they watch people of today struggling with the basic tasks of yesteryear.

Reading Diaries as Primary Sources

By reading diaries as documents, and plumbing them for all they are worth, students learn a great deal about history. For teaching the colonial period I like to use extracts from the diaries of Samuel Sewall (1652–1730) of Massachusetts and William Byrd II (1674–1744) of Virginia. Although neither man lived through the Revolution, these two diarists exemplify much about prominent men during the colonial era, and provide a useful way to contrast lifestyles in the North and South. William Byrd's plantation home still stands and can be visited today in Virginia. Neither man expected that his diary would be published. Sewall's diary was not published until the nineteenth century. Students never fail to be intrigued by the fact that Byrd wrote his in a secret code and that it was not decoded and published until 1941.

Samuel Sewall was a judge during the Salem witchcraft trials who later repented his role in the convictions. Whereas Sewall wrote one of the early tracts condemning slavery, William Byrd II owned a plantation of nearly thirty thousand acres worked by slaves along the James River in Virginia.

Gender roles, race, religion, and politics—all of these are illuminated in little more than a page of excerpts from each diary, and students enjoy reading them.

From the Diary of William Byrd II

October 28 [1709]

I rose at 6 o'clock but read nothing because Colonel Randolph came to see me in the morning. I neglected to say my prayers but I ate milk for breakfast. Colonel Harrison's vessel came in from Madeira and brought abundance of letters and among the rest I had ten from Mr. Perry with a sad account of tobacco. We went to court but much time was taken up in reading our letters and not much business was done. About 3 we rose and had a meeting of the College in which it was agreed to turn Mr. Blackamore out from being master of the school for being so great a sot...

Dec. 27 [1709]

I rose at 5 o'clock and read a chapter in Hebrew and some Greek in Cassius. I said my prayers and ate milk for breakfast. I danced my dance. When the company came down I ate chocolate likewise with them. Then we played at billiards... About 12 o'clock we went to Mr. Harrison's notwithstanding it was extremely cold and I ate some goose. In the afternoon we were very merry by a good fire till 5 o'clock. Then we returned home, where I found all well, thank God. In the evening we played at cards till about 10 o'clock and I lost a crown. I neglected to say my prayers and had good health, good thoughts, and good humor, thanks be to God Almighty.

July 15 [1710]

About 7 o'clock the Negro Betty that ran away was brought home. My wife against my will caused little Jenny to be burned with a hot iron, for which I quarreled with her. It was so hot today that I did not intend to go to the launching of Colonel Hill's ship...

Feb. 5 [1711]

I rose about 8 o'clock and found my cold still worse. I said my prayers and ate milk and potatoes for breakfast. My wife and I quarreled about her pulling her brows. She threatened she would not go to Williams-burg if she might not pull them; I refused, however, and got the better of her, and maintained my authority...

Dec. 30 [1711]

I rose about 7 o'clock and read a chapter in Hebrew and three chapters in the Greek Testament. I said my prayers very devoutly and ate boiled milk for breakfast. The weather was very clear and warm so that my wife walked out with Mrs. Dunn and forgot dinner, for which I had a little quarrel with her and another afterwards because I was not will-ing to let her have a book out of the library...

December 31 [1711]

I rose at 7 o'clock and read a chapter in Hebrew and six leaves in Lu-cian... My wife and I had a terrible quarrel about whipping Eugene while Mr. Mumford was there but she had a mind to show her author-ity before company but I would not suffer it, which she took very ill... it spoiled the mirth of the evening, but I was not conscious that I was to blame in that quarrel.

From the Diary of Samuel Sewall

January 13 [1677]

Giving my chickens meat, it came to my mind that I gave them noth-ing save Indian corn and water, and they eat it and thrived very well, and that food was necessary for them, how mean soever, which much affected me and convinced what need I stood in of spiritual food, and that I should not nauseate daily duties of prayer, &c.

July 8 [1677]

New meeting house... In sermon time there came in a female Quak-er, in a canvas frock, her hair disheveled and loose like a periwig, her face as black as ink, led by two other Quakers, and two other[s] fol-

lowed. It occasioned the greatest and most amazing uproar I ever saw. Isaiah I. 12, 14.

Nov. 12 [1685]

…The ministers of this town come to the court and complain against a dancing master who seeks to set up here and hath mixed dances, and his time of meeting is Lecture-Day; and 'tis reported he should say that by one play he could teach more divinity than Mr. Willard or the Old Testament. Mr. Moodey said 'twas not a time for N[ew] E[ngland] to dance…

Dec. 21 [1696]

A very great snow is on the ground. I go in the morn to Mr. Willard to entreat him to choose his own time to come and pray with little Sarah. He comes a little before night, and prays very fully and well… This day I remove poor little Sarah into my bed-chamber, where, about break of day Dec. 23, she gives up the ghost in nurse Cowell's arms. Born, Nov. 21, 1694. Neither I nor my wife were by, nurse not expecting so sudden a change, and having promised to call us… Nurse did long and pathetically ask our pardon that she had not called us and said she was surprised. Thus this very fair day is rendered foul to us by reason of the general sorrow and tears in the family…

May 29 [1720]

God having in his holy Sovereignty put my wife out of the fore-seat [his wife died on May 26], I apprehended I had cause to be ashamed of my sin, and to loathe myself for it; and retired into my pew… I put up a note to this purpose: Samuel Sewall, deprived of his wife by a very sudden and awful stroke, desires prayers that God would sanctify the same to himself, and children, and family…

Sept. 5 [1720]

Going to son Sewall's I there meet with Madam Winthrop, told her I was glad to meet her there, had not seen her a great while; gave her Mr. Homes's sermon.

Oct. 1 [1720]

Saturday. I dine at Mr. Stoddard's; from thence I went to Madam Winthrop's just at three. Spake to her, saying my loving wife died so soon and suddenly, 'twas hardly convenient for me to think of marrying again; however, I came to this resolution, that I would not make my court to any person without first consulting with her...

Oct. 6 [1720]

A little after six P.M. I went to Madam Winthrop's. She was not within. I gave Sarah Chickering, the maid, two shillings, Juno, who brought in the wood, one shilling. Afterward the nurse came in; I gave her eighteen pence, having no other small bill... Madam seemed to harp upon the same string. Must take care of her children; could not leave that house and neighborhood where she had dwelt so long.

Before looking at the content of the diaries, I like students to focus on their format. Each diary entry is dated. How many years do they cover? Since these are just excerpts from the diaries I want students to realize that they do not know just how many entries either man wrote in a given year. Nonetheless, the diary excerpts convey the sense of the quotidian life of each man, his tasks, hobbies, and concerns. As historian Steven Stowe (2002) comments on the History Matters website, "Diaries are shaped by moments of inspiration, but also habit."

Then there is the question of language. Only those who are literate write diaries, so historians know more about the educated classes than about the illiterate. What words or expressions are unfamiliar to our twenty-first century ears? I like students to make a list of these so we can discuss them. They include terms like *periwig*, *shilling*, *'tis*, and *'twas*. We don't much talk of "rising" in the morning, rather we get out of bed. We do not "make court," we date. Nor would any of us be likely to write, "A fair day is rendered foul." That the use of language changes over time is in itself a valuable history lesson, but it is especially important to emphasize this in the context of asking students to write diaries that sound authentic. Students need to adopt the more formal language of the eighteenth century as much as possible and forego the use of modern slang; even words like *okay* sound out of place.

Before we look closely at details in these diaries, I want students to identify major themes or story lines. William Byrd and his wife do not get along and there are disputes over who has authority. Samuel Sewall's wife dies and he quickly goes a-courting another woman. In class or for homework I ask students to make generalizations supported by evidence from the text by responding to prompts like, "What details can you find to support the hypothesis that William Byrd was well-educated and wealthy?" (he knew Ancient Greek, Latin, and Hebrew, he had leisure time, and he owned slaves) and, "How do we know that William Byrd's slaves felt unhappy and oppressed?" (there are frequent references to beatings and one slave runs away). I also pose a series of questions that ask students to compare life in the North and the South, such as, "Using the diaries as evidence, which section of the country was more deeply religious at this time, North or South?" The diaries also illuminate the role of women at this time. Some of my students speculated that Byrd's wife resented her inferior status and took out her anger on her slaves. Students are often surprised that Madam Winthrop was not so eager to remarry. Students can use the diaries to think about such questions as, What status did women hold in colonial times and what standing did widows have that married women lacked? Much information about colonial times can be extracted from the diaries if they are read with care.

Students enjoy being history sleuths and decoding original documents. Figure 2.1 is a page from John Adams's diary written on March 5, 1773, in which he reflects on the Boston Massacre of 1770, and a transcription follows it. Adams was a lawyer who defended the king's soldiers at their trial. If students get frustrated transcribing the original—and they will—remind them that this is one of the tasks historians perform. Students may be amused at the spelling and capitalization used at this time as well as the mistakes Adams makes. After comparing their transcription to the one online at the Massachusetts Historical Society (see Appendix B), ask students if they think that Adams wrote this entry with an audience in mind other than himself. What makes them think so? When Adams refers to "my country" in 1773, do students think he is referring to Great Britain, or to a country that does not yet exist, the United States?

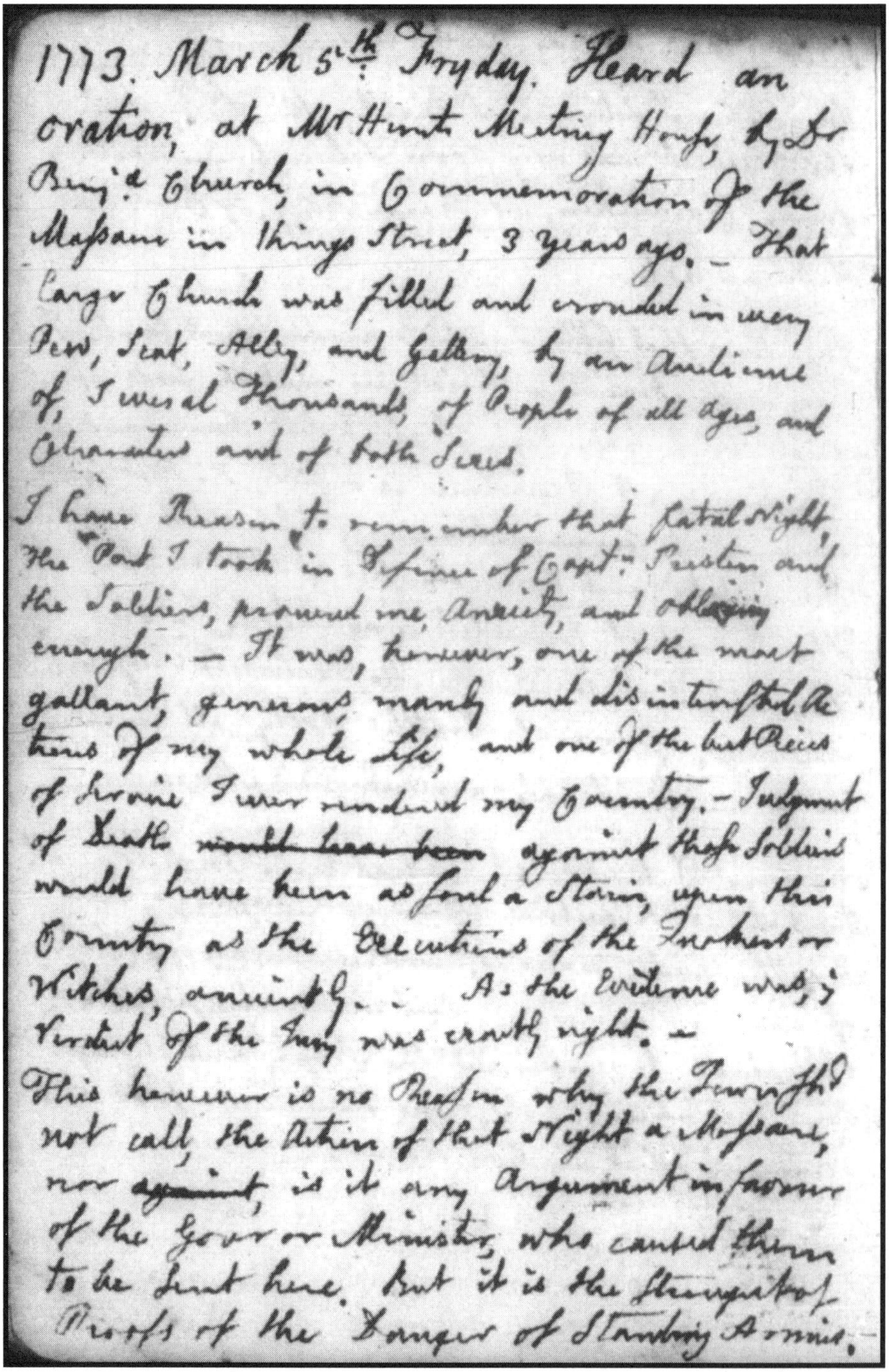

1773. March 5th Fryday. Heard an oration, at Mr Hunts Meeting House, by Dr Benja Church, in Commemoration of the Massacre in Kings Street, 3 years ago. — That large Church was filled and crowded in every Pew, Seat, Alley, and Gallery, by an Audience of, several Thousands, of People of all Ages, and Characters and of both Sexes.

I have Reason to remember that fatal Night, The Part I took in Defence of Capt. Preston and the Soldiers, procured me, Anxiety, and obloquy enough. — It was, however, one of the most gallant, generous, manly and disinterested Actions of my whole Life, and one of the best Pieces of Service I ever rendered my Country. — Judgment of Death ~~would have been~~ against those Soldiers would have been as foul a Stain, upon this Country as the Executions of the Quakers or Witches, anciently. — As the Evidence was; Verdict of the Jury was exactly right. —

This however is no Reason why the Town should not call, the Action of that Night a Massacre, nor ~~against~~, is it any Argument in favour of the Govr or Minister, who caused them to be sent here. But it is the strongest Proofs of the Danger of Standing Armies. —

Fig 2.1 John Adams reflected on the Boston Massacre in his diary.

Transcription of Adams's Diary Entry

1773. March 5th. Fryday.

Heard an Oration, at Mr. Hunts Meeting House, by Dr. Benja. Church, in Commemoration of the Massacre in Kings Street, 3 Years ago. That large Church was filled and crouded in every Pew, Seat, Alley, and Gallery, by an Audience of several Thousands of People of all Ages and Characters and of both Sexes.

I have Reason to remember that fatal Night. The Part I took in Defence of Captn. Preston and the Soldiers, procured me Anxiety, and Obloquy enough. It was, however, one of the most gallant, generous, manly and disinterested Actions of my whole Life, and one of the best Pieces of Service I ever rendered my Country. Judgment of Death ~~would have been~~ against those Soldiers would have been as foul a Stain upon this Country as the Executions of the Quakers or Witches, anciently. As the Evidence was, the Verdict of the jury was exactly right.

This however is no Reason why the Town should not call the Action of that Night a Massacre, nor ~~against,~~ is it any Argument in favour of the Governor or Minister, who caused them to be sent here. But it is the strongest of Proofs of the Danger of standing Armies.

Students Introduce Their Personas

Now that students can imagine their personas, the colony in which they lived, and the means by which they earned a livelihood, they are ready to write. To make the assignment something special I distribute composition books to students. They are inexpensive bound books with lined paper and black and white speckled cardboard covers, and they look old-fashioned right from the start. (My school keeps a big supply of these on hand for use by younger students.) Everything students write goes between the covers, giving them a feeling that they are writing something to be preserved, not merely a bunch of papers kept helter-skelter. For their first assignment I ask students to introduce themselves in the diary by explaining who they are and why they are writing. The year is 1764, one year after the end of the French and Indian War and the Proclamation of 1763 in which the British forbade the colonists from moving onto land won from France for fear of

Indian rebellions in the region.

I require that in the introductions to their diaries students must:

- Describe how and why their ancestors came to America.
- Depict life in their city, village, or rural area.
- Explain how they earn a livelihood, using details from their crafts research.
- Describe their family members, including their hopes and conflicts.
- Use vocabulary and syntax of the period, insofar as possible.

A sample of introductions written by eighth graders at the Village Community School gives a feeling for just how effectively students can recreate the period by using and thus reinforcing information previously learned about their colony and craft. All the students weave information about the colonial period acquired from their textbooks, research reports, and the supplementary primary sources we study in class.

A sample of diary entries follows. Original spelling and punctuation remain as students wrote them.

Dan, plantation owner from Maryland:

June 2nd, 1764

This first entry might seem odd, because I am not used to writing short personal pieces. The reason that I am starting this diary is that I have been offered the position of Secretary of State for Maryland. Because of the position I have decided that keeping a journal would be a good idea...

I am Sir Nathaniel Bragg of Maryland. I am a thirty-nine year old plantation owner who controls plantations throughout Maryland. But the plantation I call home is 4,000 acres large and named Bragg's Folly. It is made of four smaller tobacco plantations and while I am busy with the House of Burgesses and soon the Governor's Council, it is run by my head overseer.

My family has been in the colony of Maryland since the very beginning. In actuality one of my family members was one of the seventeen noblemen who came over with Leonard Calvert.

I am the father of four children: Daniel the oldest is now studying in Massachusetts at Harvard College, the same place that I received my education as well as my father and his father...Molly, the second oldest, is eighteen and married to the heir apparent of Tilinghams' Hope, a plantation ten miles from Bragg's Folly.

Emily, housewife from Massachusetts:

May 4, 1764

After feeding the twins, George and Mary it came to my mind about family. I started to think with pride about how my family was one of the first to settle here in Salem. My family was a well respected one for it's constant participation in the church. Later in the day I gave Mary another lesson in dyeing yarn, she cannot seem to get the knack of it. This worries me, what kind of wife will she be if she cannot do a simple thing like that?

Noah, slave from Maryland:

I was given the name Tskwade by an African man on board a slave ship. When he named me this, I was only eight years of age. Many of the people on the ship laughed at this name, but I did not know what it meant. I was born in Africa in 1737 to the wife of a merchant...When I was seven years old, I heard the screams of my mother and sister from behind the house. I ran around the back of the house, and saw three black men carrying my mother and sister off. I ran after the men, as fast as I could, but they were too quick for me, and they slipped away. I was then left to live with only my grandmother for the next year. I was filled with sorrow and grief, for who would make the patties for me to eat, and who would sing to me in the night?... Now that I am 26, I see only ever so clearly how foolish the English were. They are too foolish to work for themselves, so they must get men like us to work for them.

Michelle, midwife from Georgia

August 22, 1764

My name be Annabella Rogers. I am a mid-wife. My husband is the well-known Georgia doctor, Dr. Samuel Rogers. We have three children of beauty, Sam Younger, Elisa, and Elizabeth. This morn we all arose to work. Elisa, who is five will be knitting a sweater for her father, who is going up

North for a couple of days to study human anatomy.
Sam the younger was sent out in the woods alone by his father to hunt for
some meat for the journey. Elizabeth who is 11 years of age, helped me clean
the labor room, for today many births are expected.

Dan's entry demonstrates an excellent mastery of what he learned about Maryland and plantation life. He uses information about the founding of Maryland and knows something about its form of government. Both Dan and Noah created characters that drew on their real-life identities. Even in eighth grade Dan used to go around school in a Dartmouth College cap, determined to attend Dartmouth College like his father—just as his main character's son attends Harvard like his father did. Noah, an African American student, imagined himself a slave. In their descriptions of the slave trade and plantation life both boys drew on several primary source documents that we had read as a class, including Alexander Falconbridge's account of the slave trade and "The Interesting Narrative of the Life of Olaudah Equiano" (see Appendix B). The fact that Noah acknowledges here that Africans, too, were involved in the slave trade shows a sophisticated and accurate grasp of history.

We can see the influence of Samuel Sewall's writing on the way Emily introduced her diary. Samuel Sewall wrote, "Giving my chickens meat, it came to my mind that I gave them nothing save Indian corn and water, and they eat it and thrived very well, and that food was necessary for them, how mean soever, which much affected me and convinced what need I stood in of spiritual food." Emily begins in a similar way, with an activity that leads to a reflection: "After feeding the twins, George and Mary it came to my mind about family."

Responding to Anachronisms

Michelle's entry is not atypical of the kinds of misconceptions that students bring to their study of the past. Like Michelle, many adolescents readily learn the isolated facts in their textbooks but bring to their studies little prior knowledge with which to contextualize these facts. By imagining that Annabella's husband could go up north "for a couple of days," Michelle shows a lack of understanding of basic colonial life—it would have taken a couple of months just to travel there. She also does not realize that women gave birth in their homes and that as a midwife she would have visited them and not the reverse. It is important to address these kinds anachronisms with the class; although not all students commit them to paper, many students hold similar confusions. So rather than just correct Michelle's misconceptions privately, I bring these topics to the fore in class discussion. What kind of vehicles did the colonists use for travel? How did they practice medicine? These questions are interesting in and of themselves and the answers can range from the simple to the scholarly, depending on the level of the class.

For today's students typewriters and record players are already quaint relics of the past, but just how old are they? Many of them do not know what things were invented when or appreciate how new technologies affected lifestyles. Although students can search the Internet for time lines—and these can be very useful—a better remedy is to take class trips to historical sites whenever possible. Because my school is in New York City we visit places like the Lefferts Historic House in Brooklyn, first settled by the Dutch in the eighteenth century, or the Morris-Jumel Mansion uptown, which was Washington's headquarters for several weeks during the Revolutionary War. Being in a historic house enables students to understand—all at once—that the colonists had no indoor plumbing, electric lights, gas stoves, or telephones. At other sites we visit, such as Philipsburg Manor in Tarrytown, New York, students perform a variety of farming and cooking chores, thereby experiencing for themselves the time-consuming, complex, and labor intensive tasks that were often performed by servants or slaves.

A frequent mistake that students fall into is using modern slang expressions in their colonial diaries. The best remedy for this is exposure to literature and primary source documents of the period. It is noteworthy that Michelle tried her best to use language and syntax from the era. When she writes "my name be" she is recalling the language used in Arthur Miller's *The Crucible*, which she read in English class. Students who strive to make their diaries sound authentic invariably enjoy using words and expressions they read in primary source documents.

Illustrating the Diary Cover

While the quality of student work may vary, I want to ensure that each student puts in his or her best effort. I learned that students become more attached to their diaries and therefore produce better work when somewhere along the way they make illustrated covers for them. These are designed on separate sheets of paper cut to diary-size. Pencil, colored pencils, or watercolors look most authentic to the period. Once the cover is finished it is attached to the diary with clear plastic contact paper, giving a lovely and finished effect to the final product.

I suggest to students that they depict their home, trade, family, or self-portrait. I provide them with lots of materials to inspire ideas and to help them imagine the past and learn more about it. The Dover Coloring Book series includes *The American House: Styles of Architecture, Everyday Dress of the American Revolution,* and *Early American Trades.* I refuse to let students trace from these sources, nor are students allowed to download images from the Internet, but they can make sketches based on such sources. This is because students learn a great deal through the careful observation that is required when sketching. One student of mine, Vanessa, was brilliant at all things academic, and was used to praise. But she had no special gift for drawing and balked when asked to sketch her cover. "But I *can't* draw," she complained. My reply was, "Neither can I." I explained to her that some kids think they cannot do math either, but that does not get them out of doing math in math class. You may be able to enlist the help of an art teacher to work on the covers, saving you time and gaining valuable expertise. What is wonderful about this activity is that inevitably some artistic students have the chance to shine in an academic class.

Learning About the Revolution from Different Viewpoints

Students are now ready to start learning about the Revolution and writing about it in their diaries. To begin, I assign textbook reading and ask students to take notes on a graphic organizer. They read about and write notes on one or two events per night. Originally I formulated a chart in which the second and third columns read "American View" and "British View"—this despite the fact that there were not as yet a people known as Americans! This was a typical and oversimplified textbook point of view. In

Fig 2.2 The cover of Noah's journal depicts his knowledge of tobacco growing and its emotional and physical toll on enslaved Africans.

Fig 2.3 This cover shows that students can effectively depict what they learn about colonial lifestyles even if they are not skilled artists.

later years I revised this chart to show that some colonists supported and even fought for the Crown and that some Englishmen supported the colonists' protests. Winning the Revolution was also a struggle for hearts and minds—not just a matter of winning military battles. It is this struggle that we end up arguing in the classroom.

After students read about an event or two in their text, we discuss the event(s) in class. I supplement the textbook reading with primary source documents (see Appendix B). Fortunately, some of my early teaching was done at the City & Country School in Manhattan, whose library contained classic collections of primary source documents. Among them was *American History Told by Contemporaries,* edited by Albert Bushnell Hart in 1924. This anthology, unlike most today, includes many viewpoints and not just the winning side of a controversy. Here I found such documents as Martin Howard's "A Colonist's Defense of Taxation, 1765" and the letters of Tory Chief Justice Thomas Hutchinson of Massachusetts, which we discuss in class along with the rousing rhetoric of leaders like Patrick Henry.

Sometimes there is an apt current day parallel to fill in the last column of the graphic organizer and sometimes not, but it is always worth thinking

Event	Explanation	Rebel Colonists and Whig English	Loyal Colonists and Tory English	Current Day Parallel

about what these might be. For an interesting comparison to the Boston Massacre, ask students to interview someone who remembers the Kent State Massacre—the killing of four students by the National Guard at Kent State University during antiwar protests in 1970. Were either the guardsmen in 1970 or the British soldiers in 1770 justified in firing on a mass of demonstrators? Does each incident, which involved the killing of only a handful of people, deserve to be called a massacre? What is the emotional legacy that the deaths of only a few citizens can leave on future generations? Today the Writs of Assistance (1760), which gave citizens working on behalf of the British the power to enter homes without a warrant in search of smuggled goods, makes an interesting comparison to various provisions of the USA Patriot Act of 2001. When, if ever, should concerns about security override citizens' rights?

The chart and primary source documents help students see that there are many sides to every event leading to Revolution. Sometimes a class is ready to complete a diary assignment the same night they read about events in their texts. At other times we need to process material in class. After several years' experimentation I added a new stipulation to the diary writing.

After introducing themselves, I assigned students to take the point of view of *either* a Loyalist or a Rebel, with the class evenly divided. With this new condition in place students must write about events in their diaries *from one point of view or the other*, and consider the question, How would this latest event affect my livelihood, family, and political views? I then require that everything they say in class discussion must support their viewpoint.

Loyalists vs. Rebels: Assigning Students to Viewpoint Teams

How I determine who takes what viewpoint depends on a number of factors. Historians estimate that at the start of the Revolution one-third of the colonists remained Loyalists, one-third were ready to assert independence, and one-third were neutral or undecided. Certain historical factors do come into play when I assign teams, and we discuss these in class. Those colonists who produced manufactured goods were hurt by the British trade laws, which forbade the colonists from exporting manufactured goods. Thus I place a gunmaker, clockmaker, wigmaker, or hatmaker on the rebel side. Likewise with anyone involved in the shipping business, especially from New England. The plantation owners were divided, with many, such as Thomas Jefferson and George Washington, becoming leaders of the rebel cause. Slaves cared first and foremost about their own freedom, offered to them early in the war by the British, and only later by the rebels, if they joined their side. Printers and tavern keepers were often at the hub of rebel activity. New York was largely but not exclusively a loyalist stronghold. So history provides some guidelines as well as flexibility in assigning roles.

I also try to create evenly balanced teams in terms of student ability; both sides need passionate, smart, and hardworking students in roughly equal numbers. In general, however, it takes more sophisticated thinkers to see the Loyalist side, so I often put students who struggle to learn the basics on the side of the Rebels. I then reassign classroom seats so that Loyalists and Rebels sit on opposite sides of the room. Students are required to speak only from the viewpoint of their diarist. I learned that given this set-up, discussion quickly becomes a heated debate as I alternate calling on students from one side or the other.

The Diary Assignments

After students write their diary introductions, I give the following assignments. Each can be completed in anywhere from a one-page diary entry to several short or lengthy entries, depending on the sophistication of the students and time constraints. Each year I tweak the assignment, sometimes condensing or omitting features. The following sequence typically takes from one to two weeks to complete.

Assignment 1: 1764

In your diary write about the following:

The Navigation Acts

These laws have been in force since 1673 regulating colonial trade. Are they fair or not?

- The Loyalists think they are perfectly fair because the colonies are part of the British Empire and profit from belonging to a well-regulated system.
- The Rebels think they are unfair because they unjustly damage colonial shipping by prohibiting the production of manufactured goods.

The Writs of Assistance (1761)

- Justifiable means to search for illegally smuggled goods, or a trampling of the sacred right to privacy?

Proclamation of 1763

Is this proclamation fair or not?

- Loyalists believe the British have good reason to forbid colonists from settling west of the Appalachians. Try to imagine that you know a British soldier patrolling the region.
- Rebels believe their rights are being taken away from them. Try to imagine that you know a colonist who fought in the French and Indian War and who wants to settle in the Ohio Valley.

Personal Story Line

- Continue to develop the story of your personal life, such as marital problems, romance, illness, financial woes or benefits, and your craft or livelihood.
- Include details of sensory experiences based on colonial life, such as:
  - Smells (fireplaces, barns)
  - Sounds (chopping wood, clop of horses)
  - Touch (polished woods, soft quilts)
- Include dialogue in the form of conversations you have had with neighbors, friends, and acquaintances. Remember to think about eighteenth century language and to avoid modern slang.

Assignment 2: 1765–1766

The Stamp Act of 1765

- Do you accept this the Stamp Act as a legitimate use of Britain's rule over its citizens? Why or why not?
- If you are a Rebel, what have you done to oppose the Stamp Act? Will you purchase the stamps? What protests have you witnessed in your colony? How violent do you believe the colonists should be in their protests?
- If you are a Loyalist, what acts of protest have you witnessed against the Stamp Act? What distresses you most about seeing British law ignored and lawless citizens taking to the streets? What do you see as a solution?
- Include some further specifics about the trade or profession you practice.
- Include a clipping from a news article covering recent events. (For a discussion on analyzing newspapers as primary source documents, see Chapter 5.)

Assignment 3: 1770

The Boston Massacre

- Rebel viewpoint: The British army is here to oppress us; this is but one example.
- Loyalist viewpoint: The soldiers are here to protect us. Provoked and attacked by an unruly mob, they were forced to protect themselves.
- How did you personally learn about the events?
- Describe what you know about the trial of the soldiers and its aftermath. Do you believe justice was served? Why or why not?
- Describe your ongoing personal and work relationships. Are they being affected by political events and if so how?

Cartoon or Other Piece of Propaganda

- Include in this diary entry a cartoon that you have made which summarizes your political point of view, as does Paul Revere's engraving of the Massacre. (For a discussion about analyzing cartoons as primary source documents, see Chapter 6).

Assignment 4: 1773–1774

The Boston Tea Party (1773)

- What rumors and versions of this event have you heard?
- What do you believe really took place?
- Is the destruction of property ever justified? In your opinion, why was it justified or not justified in this case?

The Intolerable Acts (1774)

- Are the so-called Intolerable Acts a just use of British force to restore order? Why or why not?
- How have these Acts affected you personally?
- If you are a Rebel, why are you moving toward the position that King George III will never listen to the just demands of the colonists and that therefore independence is the only option? What have you done to support your views?

- If you are a Loyalist, why does it remain advantageous to remain a loyal British citizen? Why is it folly to think of independence? In your opinion, what will come of a war?

Sketch of a Scene

- Include in your diary a sketch based on daily life or on political events as you have witnessed them.

Assignment 5: 1775–1776

Lexington and Concord

- In your opinion, who fired the first shots at Lexington? Does it matter?
- Describe what you will do as war breaks out. For which side will you fight? Or will you remain neutral? Will you leave America for Canada or England? Explain your choice.
- Describe the effect of ongoing events on every member of your family. Are there family disputes over unfolding events? If so, what are they and what is their cause? How might they be resolved?

The Declaration of Independence (1776)

- Does the Declaration of Independence provide a new foundation for self-government based upon democratic principles, or is it an act of high treason that will bring chaos and defeat?

Personal Prospects

- In a war, how might your expertise in a craft or livelihood prove useful?
- How will family members fare?
- What is likely to happen in your colony in terms of defense and warfare?

Extracts from Student Diaries

Extracts from student diaries demonstrate how they incorporated fact into fiction as they developed and presented their viewpoints. In his diary, Dan has stayed very much in the character of Loyalist Nathaniel

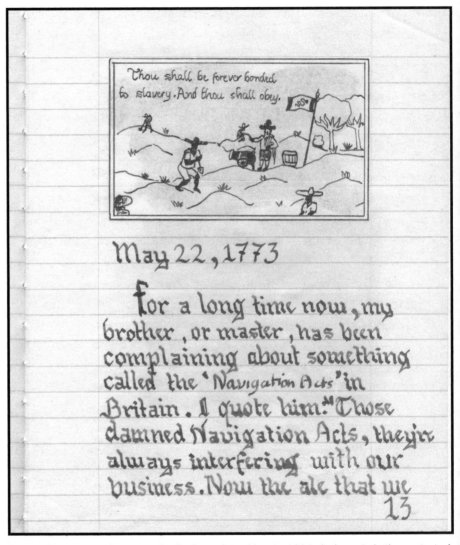

Fig 2.4 This excerpt from a student's diary relates important historical events in the context of an imagined life story.

Bragg, whom he developed in his introduction. In this entry he draws on primary sources we read that described the attack on Governor Thomas Hutchinson's home in order to imagine what might have happened to his character. We feel Bragg's personal sense of injustice when his carriage is attacked by a mob. In the dialogue Dan is trying to defend the argument for the virtual representation of the colonies in Parliament. In class discussion Dan argued this case vigorously. The news clipping he wrote and includes in his diary gives the events he describes further credibility. Student spellings and punctuation have been retained in these extracts, as they are throughout this book.

July 11, 1764

Why won't they all just politely be silent about how much they all hate the Stamp Act? Every Whig in the bloody state is up in arms complaining, the Stamp Act isn't fair. Oh no, England has made a legitimate tax for the colonies. Lets all complain like little babies. Dear God! Why shouldn't England be able to tax her own colonies? All of the other colonies and all of England is taxed, why shouldn't we?

As if this isn't bad enough they are all up in protest as well. A few days ago I not only witnessed a protest but was attacked by protesters who decided that I was the perfect target. What happened was that I was leaving the State House in my carriage when a large protest was going on. The protesters saw that my family emblem was on the outside of the carriage and immediately attacked my carriage. After letting my horses go free and severely beating my driver and my footmen they opened the door, pulled me out of the carriage and set it on fire...

During the ball that I held in honor of my being chosen as State Secretary, Richard Henry Lee my brother in law and I had an argument over the Stamp Act.

"Nathaniel old fellow, how be you?"

"I am fine Richard."

"I was wondering what is your opinion about the Stamp Act?"

"You know my opinion. I think it's a lawful use of England's power."

"Why?"

"Because everyone in England is taxed and everyone in other colonies are taxed. Why should we be an exception?"

"But its taxation without representation."

"No its taxation with representation because Parliament represents all of us."

With that I walked away from Richard who mysteriously avoided the reception line at the end of the Ball...

Below is Dan's enclosed news clipping, which was typed rather than handwritten and which he yellowed with tea to make it look old.

Annapolis Journal, July 3rd, 1764

Yesterday, right outside the State House Sir Nathaniel Bragg, an outspoken supporter of the Stamp Act, was attacked by an unruly mob. Shouting "down with the Stamp Act" over and over again they beat Sir Nathaniel's driver and both his footmen. They also burned Sir Nathaniel's carriage. Sir Nathaniel escaped unharmed but lost over £200 in property. He has put out a £50 reward for the heads of the ringleaders.

Jeannie writes her diary as a Rebel printer in New York. She is right that there was also a minor version of the Tea Party in New York, although the year was 1774. She correctly imagines the instrumental role that printers played in disseminating the ideas that led to the Revolution. Her diary beautifully captures the vagaries of life that lead ordinary people to participate, or not to participate, in historical events.

October 11, 1773

I have come down with an awful cold, and I fear I cannot attend work for at least a week. Meanwhile, Sam Adams has led the Boston Tea Party. I first learned about this event approximately two weeks ago, a week before it happened. The Mercury, being a rebellious newspaper, had pamphlets left in the printing room for anyone to take. At around that time I saw similar pamphlets planning a Tea Party for New York. I wouldn't miss this protest for the world. Unfortunately, my wife demanded that I stay home. She said "With your dreadful cold, it is not the time for you to be on the seas on a cold night, dumping tea. There are plenty of other men to accomplish this. Besides, you are a man of fifty-six years of age." And I told her, "You are never too old to be a rebel."

Deep down I know she is right. I cannot participate tonight, because I will surely catch a fatal disease. I must recline to my chamber immediately. To heal my ailment I must have some cider to calm my nerves.

In Arthur's diary we see the war approaching as he imagines it through his persona, a Loyalist silversmith living in Rhode Island. He does not assume the war can be won, nor does he gloss over the toll the Revolution will exact in terms of lives.

January 29, 1774

I can only hope that the Parliament will smarten up, for rumors of war are spreading and I like not the sound of war. Many of my neighbors in the town have already started to organize arms in case of war. Many of my neighbors are quite ready to rebel. I am deeply disappointed in Benjamin, for today Abby spotted him with little John Williams throwing stones at a British soldier who was simply passing through. How has Matthew Williams done such a terrible job in raising his child?

July 1, 1776

Providence is practically deserted, except for women and children. Many of the men have gone to Boston to fight. I am worried for the children of the men who are warring, for many will be fatherless after the fighting has ended... Most everyone from Providence fought on Breed's Hill with the patriots. Stephen Hopkins, Rhode Island's delegate, is a drunken disgrace of a man. He is old and will go along with anything as long as he can have his whisky. I know he will vote for independence, but I do not believe that it will come.

Sharing What Students Learn

Class Discussion

Class discussion takes on new dimensions when students arrive in class with their eyewitness diaries in hand. I insist that they stay in persona, representing in discussion the views and experiences of their characters. Events are fresh in their minds, vivid in their imaginations. I encourage and sometimes require them to read extracts from their diaries out loud to support their viewpoints. For example, Arthur told the class, "The Boston Port Bill is especially causing me trouble with my business. The British closed the port in Boston with a naval blockade so no ships can get in our out. This is affecting the whalers of my town… Our whole town is losing money. " Other students argued just as vociferously that the colonists had brought such a situation on their own heads. Students could see that events had real consequences, for real people. Hearing the well-written student diaries encourages other students to write more detailed and authentic-sounding entries.

I find that formerly reticent students are often eager to speak up in this situation. I believe there are several reasons for this. First, some students are simply relieved to be assigned a viewpoint for which other students will not hold them personally accountable. Such was the case with Bryony, a sophisticated thinker who always saw two sides to a controversy from the start. This often left her frozen—which was the right or wrong opinion to adopt? Rather than decide, she remained quiet. With her viewpoint assigned to her she could bring the full force of her extraordinary reasoning powers to defend it. For all students it is helpful to have formulated their arguments and opinions ahead of time and articulated them in their diaries. This gives shy students something to draw on in discussion. They can bring to our discussions of subsequent events ideas formulated in their earlier entries.

For all students the controversies leading to Revolution become more complex than they anticipate. The effect of the eyewitness perspective does not lead, however, to a diminished admiration for the generation of the Founders; quite the contrary. Because students gain a deeper appreciation of the time period, they acquire a better understanding of what was at stake in the Revolution.

Role-Plays and Simulations

A number of simulation activities follow naturally from the diary writing or can be inserted as it progresses. These include staging a trial of the soldiers in the Boston Massacre as it unfolds or ending the diary entry sequence with a simulation in which the Second Continental Congress debates whether or not to adopt the Declaration of Independence. Another simulation I developed takes a different tack. With all the talk nowadays of tax reduction students often simply label taxes as being bad, without understanding the principle of "no taxation without representation." One year I decided I had to make students *feel* the injustice of being taxed without their consent, and that is exactly what I did to them as teacher—charged them for all sorts of classroom supplies (some of which I never purchased) and demanded they themselves earn the money to pay for them (Schur 1992). They quickly felt outraged. Only by making what happened to the colonists happen to them did they begin to understand the principles at stake.

Asking What If?

A way to conclude a study of the Revolution is to ask the question, What if the Loyalists had won? Would the ideals brought to fruition by the Revolution have died an early death? Would we today be part of Canada, a member of the British Commonwealth? In *What Ifs? of American History* (2003), Caleb Carr speculates to a different effect. He asks, What if Britain had made the reforms requested by colonists, thus avoiding the need for war? He concludes, "The power of progressive constitutional thought would have been doubled, rather than dissipated; and humanity would have been far the better for it" (21). What if? questions open up history to new interpretations and engage students because even though the events happened in the past, their relevance and reinterpretation are ongoing matters in which students can still participate. Students also want to pursue the questions they have about *what did* happen to the Loyalists, a topic little discussed in textbooks.

Adapting the Eyewitness Diary Strategy

There are a few important components of the eyewitness diary assignment that make it easily transferrable to other time periods in history. I once adapted this assignment for sixth graders who were learning about the Great Irish Famine of the 1840s. Each student started off by owning a small farm in Ireland and witnessed the devastating effects as both nature and governmental policy wreaked havoc on their lives. Emigration to America was the last writing assignment. A more sophisticated version of this assignment would have included students assigned to write from a variety of perspectives: a large landowner, a member of the British Parliament, a newspaper writer, and so on.

A good eyewitness diary sequence ends with some climax, such as the outbreak of the Civil War, the Stock Market crash of 1929, or the March on Washington in 1963. Students should have roles to play within a certain historical framework. A series of events must unfold so that students are required to react to them in character. Finally, students should read a contemporaneous primary source diary on which they can model their own entries. To choose a good sequence, review a unit from the textbook and single out key events for students to write about. Then go in search of primary source documents that present multiple viewpoints.

One eyewitness diary sequence would have students debate the advisability of going to war with Mexico in 1846. This topic would resonate with questions Americans ask themselves today about whether we were justified in going to war with Iraq. On the side in favor of going to war with Mexico belong American settlers living in the Republic of Texas, slaveholders, and small farmers in search of land. On the antiwar side belong Easterners, abolitionists, slaves, and Mexicans. Questions students can consider include, Were the charges for war trumped up by Polk? and What if the United States had never acquired Texas and California, both taken from Mexico by the war's end? In the textbook that I use these events cover about twenty pages—and the material is not much fun for students to study and memorize straight-up. After incorporating information in an eyewitness diary, however, students need to do less studying for tests, not more. After all, how hard is it to memorize events that you yourself have "lived" through?

Assessment

Among the many advantages of the eyewitness diary assignment is the reciprocal relationship between what students write at home and what we discuss in class. Students who need time to formulate their ideas can do so on paper first. Everyone comes prepared with something to say and a point of view to contribute. This generates tremendous excitement in the classroom. Assessing student performance in discussion is thus an important aspect of this work.

A rubric like the one that follows is useful for evaluating all the work a student has completed for the eyewitness diary assignment or for evaluating a piece of the project they have submitted from their portfolio. Of course, I also give a test on the American Revolution with many short answer questions and several essay questions. I am always exceedingly pleased by how well students perform on it. After writing the diary assignments, students understand why events unfolded the way they did. Their grasp of chronology (and especially of causal relationships) is very strong. They also come away with a deep understanding of the issues at stake in the American Revolution.

Rubric for Student Diaries

Topic	Criteria	Mark from 1–5
Writing, Technical	Spelling, grammar, punctuation, syntax, proofreading	
Writing, Artistic	Do you write in the first-person, present tense? Do you provide vivid and accurate factual details? Do you provide sensory descriptions (sights, sounds, smells)? Is the vocabulary rich, varied, and appropriate to the time period?	
Historical Content: Events	Do you incorporate historical events into your narrative, as per instructions? Do you include facts and relevant detail? Do you provide an ongoing rationale for your viewpoint about these events?	
Historical Content: Lifestyle	Do you write about your livelihood and home life with historical accuracy for the time period? Does your narrative evolve in a credible manner?	
Artwork: Cover and Inserts (including news clip, cartoon, sketch)	Does your cover reveal effort? Does it reflect historical accuracy? Is it artistically pleasing? Do your inserts reflect appropriate content? Do they reflect effort?	
Class Discussion	Did you contribute regularly to class discussion? Did you effectively represent your side's viewpoint of the conflict?	
Overall Comment		

Chapter Three

Travelogues: Eyewitness Perspectives on a Growing Nation

From the city of New York to the Plains of Mexico is a stride that I myself can scarcely realize.

Susan Magoffin, Independence, Missouri, 1846

Explorers, missionaries, naturalists, migrants, settlers, and journalists have all been eager to report on where they have been and what they have seen for those of us never likely to go ourselves. Because readers want to envision what they cannot see, travelogues throughout history often have been accompanied by illustrations and, more recently, by photographs. Travel accounts thus provide vivid models from which students can write and illustrate their own imaginary journeys set in whatever period of American history you choose. The travelogue assignment creates wonderful opportunities to study geography and to integrate art, English, and social studies.

The value of this eyewitness strategy is that it helps students integrate the fact that America encompassed vastly different landscapes, peoples, and lifestyles within the same time frame. A great amount of information from students' textbooks can be synthesized and brought to life through their own eyewitness accounts. Similar to the diary assignment, a travelogue is organized chronologically, but rather than record their reactions to a series of historical events, students write about what they see on each stop as the journey proceeds. What they think about what they see depends upon the persona they create for themselves and thus emphasizes point of view.

To write a travelogue, students must have models on which to base their own. Early in the school year I always assign excerpts from Thomas Hariot's *A Briefe and True Report of the New Found Land of Virginia* about the ill-fated colony of Roanoke. The 1590 edition (available with illustrations on the Web; see Appendix C) was published with engravings of the drawings by John White, leaving us with a visual as well as written account of the flora, fauna, and native populations of what is today the Outer Banks of North Carolina. The book was published so that the English would not lose heart with the difficulties of planting a colony in America, "So that you may generally know & learn what the country is & thereupon consider how our dealing therein is to proceed, [how the venture] may return you profit and gain; be it either by inhabiting & planting." Hariot's book points out a deficit to using travel accounts in the classroom: imperialism and travel writing often went hand in hand. We know what Europeans thought of the natives, but not what the natives thought of them. Nonetheless, we have no better record of the Croatoan Indians encountered by Hariot and White than the record these Europeans left us.

After the settlement of America and the founding of a democratic nation, a new wave of European writers continued to visit in the 1830s and 1840s, eager to report firsthand about the American experiment. Alexis de Tocqueville is the most prominent of these, but others include the English authors Charles Dickens, Mrs. Frances Trollope (mother of novelist Anthony Trollope), social theorist Harriet Martineau, and the British actress and abolitionist Fanny Kemble. Writing about the American scene in the antebellum period were Mark Twain, the landscape architect Frederick Law Olmstead (then a reporter who toured the South), and Richard Henry Dana, whose *Two Years Before the Mast* (1841) described life at sea as well as in California. American authors include those who continued to explore or settle the West, such as Lewis and Clark and Francis Parkman. Each visitor had a particular purpose and point of view in undertaking the journey and

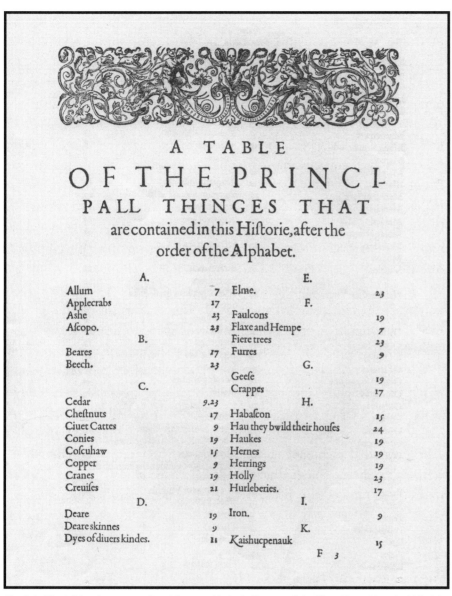

Fig 3.1 The table of contents from Thomas Hariot's *Report of the New Found Land of Virginia* reveals the extent to which the explorers were interested in resources for prospective colonists.

writing about it. As both literature and history these accounts provide teachers with excellent sources of information and models of outstanding travel writing. Publication details of these and other travelogues are found in Appendix C.

By reading travelogues students can study the settlement of the Far West and its effect on native peoples and Mexicans. But the vast majority of primary accounts are written from the viewpoint of the vanquishers, not the vanquished. In *Teaching Tolerance* (2006) Ken Olsen suggests reversing point of view when teaching about the travels of Lewis and Clark by asking students to keep a journal from the point of view of York, William Clark's slave, or Sacajawea, the Shoshone woman who helped guide them. Historians have collected the diaries of many women making the westward journey in wagon trains, and these diaries make excellent primary sources to give students. The Gold Rush brought visitors from all around the world, and Americans reached the gold fields using a variety of overland and sea routes. Students can imagine themselves as a variety of individuals en route for various reasons, including Chinese immigrants, although there are few accounts left by the Chinese themselves.

Other migrant stories that can be documented as travelogues include the Great Migration of African Americans south to north from roughly 1910 through World War II. During the Great Depression Americans from all backgrounds dispersed around the country in search of work, traveling in boxcars and piling into automobiles. Students can envision themselves as displaced Okies traveling to California, workers hired by the Tennessee Valley Authority (TVA), or journalists and photographers like Dorothea Lange who documented what they saw as they traveled cross country. Jack Kerouac's semi-autobiographical work *On the Road* (1959) gives students of the 1950s one writer's take on America at half-century. John Steinbeck wrote *Travels with Charley in Search of America* (1962) in the following decade.

Travelogues and the Textbook

The first thing I decide when setting up a travelogue assignment is the period I want to cover. My favorite era for this assignment is the antebellum period up to 1850.

Student itineraries extend from the eastern seaboard to the Mississippi River basin, giving them a taste of the rural South with its slave-based economy, the industrial North with its influx of immigrant workers, and the thrust of Americans moving westward and their impact on native populations. The United States was expanding and the question of whether or not slavery would expand westward became a hot issue. Not only were different regions of America geographically and culturally distinct from one another, but new modes of transportation changed how people traveled and where they went. The stagecoach followed a variety of national roads paved in up-to-date macadam, canals facilitated east-west travel as rivers were connected, and steam powered both ships and railroads. To integrate all of this information in a meaningful way can be both daunting and fun. To start with, students need to learn the borders of the United States within which they will imagine their travels and must be able to distinguish the states from the territories. Providing students with a historical map is thus a good way to start.

A great deal of the information students need to complete their travelogues usually appears in their textbooks (including maps of canals, roads, railways, and river systems). I always supplement this material with examples from primary source documents. According to John S. Whitley and Arnold Goldman in their introduction to the 1972 reissue of Charles Dickens's *American Notes* (1842), British travelers to America wrote over two hundred books between 1815 and 1860.

A good way for students to get an overview of what fascinated both American and foreign travel writers is to provide them with the opening page and table of contents of a variety of travel accounts. Mrs. Trollope's table of contents lists, "Chapter 1: Entrance of the Mississippi—Balize," "Chapter 2: New Orleans—Society—Creoles and Quadroons—Voyage up the Mississippi," "Chapter 3: Company on Board the Steam-Boat—Scenery of the Mississippi—Crocodiles—Arrival at Memphis—Nashoba," and on up river through Cincinnati, Philadelphia, New York, and Niagara Falls. I ask students to plot her journey using her table of contents and to make deductions about what interested her and why.

A Sample Travelogue Assignment

A sample of a travelogue assignment set in the antebellum period follows.

Directions to Students

You must use four means of transportation to travel among four of the cities listed below while visiting the Northeast, South, and West. Look at a variety of maps of the time period to plot your journey. First note the various natural and man-made ways these cities were connected. Then figure out which modes of transportation you will use to travel from one place to the next. Mark your itinerary on a map to include in your travelogue.

Cities to Visit	Modes of Transportation
1. Baltimore	1. Stagecoach
2. Boston	2. Canal boats
3. Cleveland	3. Railroads
4. New Orleans	4. Riverboats (flatboats and keelboats)
5. New York City	5. Steamboats
6. Richmond	
7. St. Louis	
8. Washington, D.C.	

(Note: If you want students to learn about the city in which they live you can always include that in your itinerary and harness the local historical society to help your students do research.)

For each region you visit discuss at least two of the topics listed below. Include a minimum of one drawing or sketch of something you have seen in each region you visit.

The West
- Religious revival and camp meetings
- American Indian nations
- Migrants from the East and South
- Spread of slavery
- Growth of new cities

The Northeast
- Industrial growth, factories in cities such as Lowell, Massachusetts
- Educational reform movements

- Early trade unions
- Immigrant groups
- Abolitionist movement
- Transcendentalist writers
- Institutions for the poor and the insane

The South

- Effect of the cotton gin
- Plantation life (including cotton, rice, sugar, and tobacco)
- Slave auctions
- Slave uprisings

Choosing a Persona

Before you write, decide who you are, where you are from, and the purpose of your journey. A list of possibilities follows. Note that some of these would of necessity be white males (congressman) while other categories could include women and African Americans (temperance organizer, school reformer, abolitionist, and preacher).

Possible Personas

- An abolitionist
- A congressman from the frontier
- A proslavery politician
- A temperance organizer
- An itinerant preacher
- A newly arrived immigrant
- A land speculator
- A railroad developer
- A school, prison, or hospital reformer
- An actor or actress on tour
- An organizer for the underground railroad
- A representative of an Indian nation en route to Washington
- A scientist, inventor, or naturalist

Writing Your Travelogue

You will write your travelogue in a composition book that I will give you. For each entry, provide a date and your location at the time you are writing. Paste the map and your sketches as you complete them into the composition book.

As a travel writer your goal is to write as vividly as possible. Your reader wants to experience what you experience, so describe what you see, hear, feel, taste, and smell in detail. Describe your encounters with famous individuals living at this time and include interviews with "the common" man or woman and people in the street.

In your conclusion, provide your persona's viewpoints about life in America at this time. Include a comparison of the Northeast, South, and West and your assessment of America as a whole. Did your journey meet your expectations?

Assigning the Work

Most textbooks alternate chapters on politics (elections, wars, and so on) with chapters on social history (lifestyles, economic developments, cultural life, etc.). Before giving the assignment, I scan our textbook to make sure there is a lot in it for students to use. I can then rest assured that they will learn the material in the process of incorporating it into their own imagined journeys. It is the chapters on social history that are most relevant to the travelogue. I use these as a jumping-off point for the types of things students will write about and see on their journeys. While "visiting" any of the regions, students can write about cultural events such as concerts and plays, religion and church attendance, hospitals, the role of women, relationships among different social classes and races, the political scene, the temperance movement, and so forth.

The assignment itself is spread over approximately two weeks during which time I specify which pages in their texts students should read and how many legs of the journey they should write about. Students can further investigate specific cities and sights using current or historical travel guides, books, and the Internet.

Inherent in travel writing is a comparison—what the writer sees on the journey compared to what he or she has seen before. Typically, whatever the writer's home base is like is viewed as the norm, while things and people encountered on the journey are viewed as different and exotic. According to M. E. Lorcin, whose essay "Women's Travel Writing" (2003–2005) appears on the website of George Mason University,

> I begin [my classes] by discussing two concepts pertinent to travel writing: the other *and the* gaze. *Both are essential to understanding the way difference is construed, whether that difference is one of gender, race, nation, or culture. The* other *is the antithesis of the self and therefore serves an accentual purpose in the conceptualization of the* self. *The* gaze, *on the other hand, is the way a particular group, conditioned by its gender, national allegiance, social standing or professional class, views the world.*

In the opening to *Roughing It*, published in 1872, Mark Twain tells us that his motives for undertaking a journey to the Far West were inspired by his romanticized images of what he expected to see. Reading it with students gives them a good opportunity to share information about where they themselves have traveled so far in their lives, what motivated them to go, and how the purpose of the journey affected their perceptions of what they saw. Students enjoy Mark Twain's sardonic humor and the way he depicts sibling rivalry. Twain is so eager to go west that he does not mind being undersecretary to his older brother, not an enviable position for a younger sibling!

From Mark Twain's *Roughing It*

> *My brother had just been appointed Secretary of Nevada Territory—an office of such majesty that it concentrated in itself the duties and dignities of treasurer, comptroller, secretary of state and acting governor in the governor's absence. A salary of eighteen hundred dollars a year and the title of "Mr. Secretary" gave to the great position an air of wild and imposing grandeur. I was young and ignorant, and I envied my brother. I coveted his distinction and his financial splendor, but particu-*

larly and especially the long, strange journey he was going to make, and the curious new world he was going to explore. He was going to travel! I never had been away from home, and that word "travel" had a seductive charm for me. Pretty soon he would be hundreds and hundreds of miles away on the great plains and deserts, and among the mountains of the Far West, and would see buffaloes and Indians, and prairie dogs, and antelopes and have all kinds of adventures, and maybe get hanged or scalped, and have ever such a fine time, and write home and tell us about it, and be a hero…What I suffered in contemplating his happiness, pen cannot describe. And so, when he offered me, in cold blood, the sublime position of private secretary under him… my contentment was complete. At the end of an hour or two I was ready for the journey. Not much packing up was necessary, because we were going in the overland stage from the Missouri frontier to Nevada, and passengers were only allowed a small quantity of baggage apiece. There was no Pacific railroad in those fine times of ten or twelve years ago—not a single rail of it. (1872)

Exercises for Understanding Point of View

A good way to help students develop their persona and understand how writers' viewpoints affect what they recount is to ask students to put themselves in the place of travelers in their own school. I take the class, their papers and pens in hand, to view one location in my school and ask them to write about it from different vantage points. For example, one group of students can write about the school yard while looking down on it from the school roof, another from across the street, while a third is stationed inside the school yard itself. Alternatively, I take the entire class to the lunchroom and ask them to describe what they see from the point of view of a school janitor, cook, student, or teacher. It is fun to compare these accounts afterward. Everyone witnesses the same scene, but the details they focus on are very different.

Now that students understand what it means to write from an eyewitness viewpoint they are ready to analyze point of view in primary source documents. I ask them to compare four eyewitness accounts of travel by steamboat in antebellum America. I give students biographical information about the authors (see the following list), but not who wrote which account. Their task is to match each description to its author and to list all the pieces of evidence that convinced them their match is correct. This guessing game demands careful reading of the documents for clues, and it never fails to engage their interest. I then ask students to write a statement about how steamboats worked and the pros and cons of traveling on them based on information gained from all four accounts. Students will learn a lot from the descriptions of the boats if they try to sketch them based on what the authors say.

Biographical Information Handout

- Charles Dickens (1812–1870) is the world-famous British author who wrote *Oliver Twist*, *A Tale of Two Cities*, and many other novels that were enormously popular in Britain and America in his day. The purpose of his five-month tour was to write a book about his impressions of America. He published *American Notes* in 1842.
- Mrs. Frances Trollope (1799–1863) is the mother of the famous British novelist Anthony Trollope. She moved to America with her three children to make money by opening a store in the Midwest. When the store failed she traveled for fifteen months around the country. Her account *Domestic Manners of the Americans* was published in 1832.
- Mark Twain (1835–1910) grew up in Hannibal, Missouri, and later became a steamboat captain, journalist, and author of *The Adventures of Tom Sawyer* and *Adventures of Huckleberry Finn*. In 1883 he published *Life on the Mississippi*, in which he describes growing up on the Mississippi River in the 1840s.
- George Catlin (1796–1872) was a lawyer turned artist who was born in Wilkes Barre, Pennsylvania. He was inspired to travel west in order to document Indians and their culture in his art. His paintings, called the Indian Gallery, toured America.

Primary Source Exercise: Four Travelers Describe the Steamboat

Charles Dickens, from *American Notes*

If the native packets I have already described be unlike anything we are in the habit of seeing on water, these western vessels are still more foreign to all the ideas we are accustomed to entertain of boats. I hardly know what to liken them to, or how to describe them.

In the first place, they have no mast, cordage, tackle, rigging or other such boat-like gear; nor have they anything in their shape at all calculated to remind one of a boat's head, stern, sides or keel…There is no visible deck, even: nothing but a long, black, ugly roof, covered with burnt-out feathery sparks; above which tower two iron chimneys, a hoarse escape-valve, and a glass steerage-house. Then, in order as the eye descends towards the water, are the sides, and doors, and windows of the state-rooms jumbled as oddly together as though they formed a small street…And in the narrow space between this upper structure and this barge's deck, are the furnace fires and machinery open at the sides to every wind that blows, and every storm of rain it drives along its path.

Passing one of these boats at night, and seeing the great body of fire…that rages and roars beneath the frail pile of painted wood: the machinery, not warded off or guarded in any way, but doing its work in the midst of the crowd of idlers and emigrants and children, who throng the lower deck: under the management, too, of reckless men whose acquaintance with its mysteries may have been of six months' standing: one feels directly that the wonder is, not that there should be so many fatal accidents, but that any journey should be safely made. ([1842] 1972, 202)

George Catlin, as excerpted from the anthology *Mirror for Americans*

The greater part of the shores of this river [the Upper Missouri], however, are without timber, where the eye is delightfully relieved by wandering over the beautiful prairies; most of the way gracefully slop-

ing down to the water's edge, carpeted with the deepest green, and, in the distance, softening into velvet of the richest hues, entirely beyond the reach of the artist's pencil…

The poor and ignorant people for the distance of 2000 miles, had never before seen or heard of a steam-boat, and in some places they seemed at a loss to know what to do or how to act…We had on board one twelve-pound cannon and three or four eight pound swivels, which we were taking up to arm the Fur Company's Fort at the mouth of Yellow Stone; and at the approach to every village they were all discharged several times in rapid succession, which threw the inhabitants into utter confusion and amazement—some of them laid their faces to the ground, and cried to the Great Spirit…some deserted their villages and ran to the tops of the bluff some miles distant…There were many curious conjectures amongst their wise men, with regard to the nature and powers of the steam-boat. Amongst the Mandans, some called it the "big thunder canoe"…it was medicine (mystery) because they could not understand it; and it must have eyes, for said they, "it sees its own way, and takes the deep water in the middle of the channel." They had no idea of the boat being steered by the man at the wheel. ([1832–1839] 1952, 514–515)

Mark Twain, from *Life on the Mississippi*

Once a day a cheap, gaudy packet arrived upward from St. Louis, and another downward from Keokuk. Before these events, the day was glorious with expectancy; after them, the day was a dead and empty thing. Not only the boys, but the whole village, felt this. After all these years I can picture that old time to myself now just as it was then: the white town drowsing in the sunshine of a summer's morning; the streets empty or pretty nearly so; one or two clerks sitting in front of the Water Street stores, with their splint-bottomed chairs tilted back against the wall, chins on breasts, hats slouched over their faces, asleep…presently a film of dark smoke appears above one of those remote "points"; instantly a negro drayman, famous for his quick eye and prodigious voice, lifts up the cry, "S-t-e-a-m-boat a-comin!"

and the scene changes! The town drunkard stirs, the clerks wake up, a furious clatter of drays follows, every house and store pours out a human contribution, and all in a twinkling the dead town is alive and moving. Drays, carts, men, boys, all go hurrying from many quarters to a common center, the wharf. Assembled there, the people fasten their eyes upon the coming boat as upon a wonder they are seeing for the first time… And the boat is a rather a handsome sight, too. She is long and sharp and trim and pretty: she has two tall, fancy-topped chimneys…a fanciful pilot house, all glass and "gingerbread," perched on top of the "texas" deck behind them; the paddle-boxes are gorgeous with a picture or with gilded rays above the boat's name; the boiler-deck…the hurricane-deck, and the texas deck are fenced and ornamented with clean white railings; there is a flag gallantly flying from the jack-staff; the furnace doors are open and the fires flaring bravely; the upper decks are black with passengers; the captain stands by the big bell, calm, imposing, the envy of all…the captain lifts his hand, a bell rings, the wheels stop…and the steamer is at rest. Then such a scramble as there is to get aboard, and to get ashore, and to take in freight and to discharge freight, all at one and the same time; and such a yelling and cursing as the mates facilitate it all with! Ten minutes later the steamer is under way again, with no flag on the jack-staff and no black smoke issuing from the chimneys. After ten more minutes the town is dead again, and the town drunkard asleep by the skids once more. ([1883] 1983, 21–22)

Mrs. Frances Trollope, from *Domestic Manners of the Americans*

The innumerable steam-boats, which are the stagecoaches and fly-wagons of this land of lakes and rivers, are totally unlike any I had seen in Europe, and greatly superior to them…The room to which the double line of windows belongs, is a very handsome apartment; before each window a neat little cot is arranged in such a manner as to give its drapery the air of a window-curtain. This room is called the gentleman's cabin, and their exclusive right to it is somewhat uncourte-

ously insisted upon. The breakfast, dinner, and supper, are laid in this apartment, and the lady passengers are permitted to take their meals there…We found the room destined for the use of the ladies dismal enough, as its only windows were below the stern gallery…

We had a full complement of passengers on board. The deck, as is usual, was occupied by the Kentucky flat-boat men, returning from New Orleans, after having disposed of the boat and cargo which they had conveyed thither, with no other labour than that of steering her, the current bringing her down at the rate of four miles an hour. We had about two hundred of these men on board; but the part of the vessel occupied by them is so distinct from the cabins, that we never saw them, except when we stopped to take in wood; and then they ran, or rather sprung and vaulted over each other's heads to the shore, when they all assisted in carrying wood to supply the steam-engine; the performance of this duty being a stipulated part of the payment of their passage… They are a most disorderly set of persons, constantly gambling and wrangling, very seldom sober…

The total want of all the usual courtesies of the table, the voracious rapidity with which the viands were seized and devoured; the strange uncouth phrases and pronunciation; the loathsome spitting, from the contamination of which it was absolutely impossible to protect our dresses; the frightful manner of feeding with their knives, till the whole blade seemed to enter in the mouth; and the still more frightful manner of cleaning the teeth afterwards with a pocket-knife, soon forced us to feel…that the dinner-hour was to be anything rather than an hour of enjoyment. ([1832] 1927, 13–15)

My students do not need help reading these accounts, although they may not understand every word. (For less able readers I would suggest that the teacher edit them into simpler sentences and provide some vocabulary words in brackets.) My class can identify Catlin by his painterly descriptions of colors and scenery and because he puts himself in the place of the natives, telling us how they thought steamboats worked by "medicine," or magic. Catlin's description emphasizes the steamboat's intrusion into the native environment. The woman among the group is the only author to remark on the segregation of the sexes on board ship. Her focus is on social interaction and social class. Twain is identifiable because he writes as a resident of America looking back on his youth growing up here. His account is tinged with the glow of nostalgia.

From the primary sources we understand how steamboats functioned to unite isolated frontier settlements. Students can identify Dickens, if not by process of elimination, then by his superior attitude toward the "native packets." His description emphasizes America's readiness to put "progress" before safety. Each author not only describes, but also presents his or her own assessment of what is seen. It is useful to point out to students how these authors use present tense to make their descriptions vivid; we too are "seeing" what they see at this very moment in time.

Getting to Know America: Researching Information to Include

Just how much time you want students to spend on research will vary. The simplest way to go about this project is to use the text as the main source of information supplemented with primary source documents. As you assign relevant chapters of the text, students pull out the information they want to incorporate into their travelogues from an eyewitness viewpoint. I also ask students to choose something about the city they are "traveling to" and research it on the Web for homework each night. This gives me the opportunity to teach about key word searches and assessing a website's reliability. One year the activity proved much more fun than I had expected. Each day I began class by asking students to share one thing they learned from a Web search. Keith, Emma, and Ramon researched different cities and websites, but all discovered that cholera was a major health threat in America in the 1830s. After Hurricane Katrina, Charles was interested in pursuing questions about New Orleans. Did they celebrate Mardi Gras in the 1830s, and if so, how?

Because students imagine themselves traveling cross-country, the travelogue provides many opportunities to teach the geography of the United States. Utilizing an atlas with a variety of types of maps of the United States, students can glean information directly relevant to their travels. Elevation maps can tell them a good deal about the ease or difficulty of traveling in specific regions, the lowest crossing point over the Appalachian or Rocky Mountains, for example. From climate maps they can deduce the likely temperatures in different sections of the country while they assess what grows there by examining vegetation maps. Further research into flora and fauna allows students to imagine what animals they might see on their journeys, from bison to grizzly bears. All of this information can be incorporated into their travelogues with a bit of braggadocio and a tall tale or two.

Regional Tour Groups

An alternative way to research material for the writing of travelogues is to divide the class into tour groups. Each group is assigned to research one form of transportation and one city to which class members will "travel." Tour groups research information and then teach the rest of the class the information they need to incorporate into their travelogues. The entire class "visits" the same sites in the same order, using the same sequence of modes of transportation. Depending upon the size of the tour group and the time I have for this activity I ask each group to produce some or all of the following items.

- A mural of their city
- A transportation display
- A travel brochure about their city and its environs
- A travel poster
- A handout of a primary source about their city

Each tour group creates a booth in one corner of the room. The art department helps my students paint murals of their cities as they looked in the assigned time period. It works well to paint the murals on very large poster board, the type with two flexible flaps on each end that students use for science fair displays; these can be easily propped up and taken down. It is important that students have copies of old paintings and maps of their cities on which to base their mural. Through observation they learn the type of architecture then in vogue, the city's relationship to its geographical setting, the state of its development, and so forth. I always ask students to point out the highest place in each city. This is invariably a church steeple, even in antebellum New York City.

Students enjoy designing flyers for their brochures and deciding what should go into them. I photocopy these when they are finished so that the tour groups can distribute them when the class visits their booth. Current or historical travel guides are good sources of information for the brochures. Students can pour through a Frommer's or Fodor's guide looking specifically for those buildings and institutions that existed in the time period they are studying. Better yet is to find old travel guides or facsimiles of them like the Baedeker guides first issued in the 1820s. I own a paperback version of *The 1866 Guide to New York City* replete with lithographs. Many of the buildings depicted still stand today, and it can be fun for students to compare the way they looked then to the way they look now.

Also useful are the guides written by the writers employed by the Federal Writers' Project during the Great Depression. These guides are great resources for a travelogue set in that period, but they are also full of history in general. These are still available in paperback for a wide array of cities and states, including New Orleans. With debate still swirling about the rebuilding of New Orleans in the aftermath of Hurricane Katrina, it is important for students to learn about the strategic and historical importance of that city in particular.

I assign a subdivision of each tour group to research one mode of transportation, such as canals, steamboats, or railroads. I require that their displays include large-scale diagrams on poster board that label their vehicle's component parts, explain how it works, and describe when and why it was invented. Students also list the advantages and disadvantages of this mode of transportation in terms of cost, comfort, speed, and safety.

I like students to understand how controversial new modes of transportation could be at the time they were introduced. The Erie Canal was branded "Clinton's ditch" by detractors who thought the idea utter folly. According to Carol Sheriff of the College of William and Mary, "Many middle-class men and women feared that the Erie Canal posed a threat to civilized society. They thought that the waterway had become a haven for vice and immorality. The towpath attracted workers who drank, swore, gambled, and worse...The biggest culprit, they believed, was the poor example they set by conducting business on the Sabbath." Likewise railroads came under attack. Included in B. A. Botkin and Alvin H. Harlow's anthology

A Treasury of Railroad Folklore (1953), one contemporary wrote in the 1830s that railroads induced "Grave, plodding citizens [to fly] about like comets. All local attachments will be at an end. It will encourage flightiness of intellect. Veracious people will turn into the most immeasurable liars; all their conceptions will be exaggerated by their magnificent notions of distance. 'Only a hundred miles off? Tut, nonsense, I'll step across, madam, and bring your fan!'" (67) Students must also search for at least one primary source document in which travelers describe their group's assigned city. They must also find contemporaneous accounts by travelers onboard whatever vehicle they have researched.

When all tour groups are ready with their materials, after approximately one week of work, we "visit" each city. The class gathers around one booth, takes a copy of its brochure, reads the displays, looks at the mural, listens to brief oral reports, and takes a photocopy of the primary sources that the group distributes. Homework over the next few nights is to incorporate into their travelogues what they learned at that city's booth. If we start off in New York City, we might travel the Erie Canal to reach Cleveland, rest in Cleveland at the "travel booth" to learn about the city and its environs, and then describe travel on a railway car to Saint Louis followed by a steamboat to New Orleans. It is important that students date their journeys to reflect the real time it would have taken to travel from place to place.

Paintings and Photographs as Primary Sources: The Postcard Assignment

Travelers on a journey do not have much time to write. They want to capture what they have seen while the memory is fresh as quickly as possible. As students start to write their travelogues I want them to feel the rush of excitement as a different world passes by. One writing assignment I start with is a postcard writing assignment. While today's technologically savvy travelers might send a text message or email with an accompanying digital photo, travelers from the 1870s on wrote (and still write) postcards. No matter the medium, the message is still the same: *See where I am!*

I begin the assignment by distributing blank 4x6 or 5x7 index cards. On one side I add a line to divide the space for the address from the space for a message, thus creating a postcard. I also distribute pictures of something scenic that students might see along their imaginary route. Each year I buy new calendars and save them for this purpose—so I can distribute a different print to each student to write about from a "see where I am" perspective. Nowadays it is easy to search the Web for appropriate works of art for students to view on the computer screen. Those by Thomas Cole, Albert Bierstadt, F. E. Church, Winslow Homer, or George Catlin work especially well. So would photographs by Timothy O'Sullivan, George Fiske, and William Henry Jackson. (If students have made murals we might sit in front of one of them instead.) I ask each student to look at his or her painting carefully. Next I ask students to put themselves into the landscape. Where are they standing or sitting as they view this scene? What sounds do they hear? What do they smell? This is a good opportunity to ask students to fill in a Photo Analysis Worksheet from the National Archives (see Figure 3.2 and Appendix H). This form works equally well for paintings and lithographs, and it helps students to "read" their visual prompts for all they are worth.

Before students start to write we discuss the *style* in which people write postcards. Travelers do not have much time to write, nor much space in which to describe things. They have to convey the maximum amount of information in the minimum amount of space. They may dispense with writing in full sentences for lack of both time and space. The writing is thus

THE U.S. NATIONAL ARCHIVES & RECORDS ADMINISTRATION
www.archives.gov   Monday, January 8, 2007

Photo Analysis Worksheet

Step 1. Observation

A. Study the photograph for 2 minutes. Form an overall impression of the photograph and then examine individual items. Next, divide the photo into quadrants and study each section to see what new details become visible.

B. Use the chart below to list people, objects, and activities in the photograph.

People	Objects	Activities

Step 2. Inference

Based on what you have observed above, list three things you might infer from this photograph.

Step 3. Questions

A. What questions does this photograph raise in your mind?

B. Where could you find answers to them?

Designed and developed by the
Education Staff, National Archives and Records Administration, Washington, DC 20408.

Page URL: http://www.archives.gov/education/lessons/worksheets/photo.html

The U.S. National Archives and Records Administration
8601 Adelphi Road, College Park, MD 20740-6001 • Telephone: 1-86-NARA-NARA or 1-866-272-6272

Fig 3.2 Photo Analysis Worksheet

condensed and even poetic. Sights, sounds, smells, climate, wildlife, human interaction—these are all things postcard writers convey. I challenge students to describe their assigned visual prompt so well that when I post all visual prompts on the bulletin board, and each student reads aloud what he or she wrote, the class can guess which message belongs with which painting and pin it on the board accordingly.

This assignment can be easily adapted to other eras—by using the photographs of Dorothea Lange or Walker Evans as visual prompts for a travelogue set in the Great Depression, for example. This little exercise provides a good warm-up to writing a sustained travelogue in which students can expand at greater length about their observations.

Rick wrote about Albert Bierstadt's painting *The Rocky Mountains, Lander's Peak* (1863) which can be viewed on the website of the Metropolitan Museum of Art. He wrote it to "My Dear Cousin Eric Waldo Romerson IV" (a sophisticated and intentional reference to Ralph Waldo Emerson!) and these are just some excerpts from his very detailed postcard.

> How are you lately? Are you well?...Are you still writing? Because the scenery is enough to spark imagination in anyone. First off, the sky. It is blue with white clouds. But they have a golden shine to them. Three of the several mountains that I see are in the clouds at their peeks...I am standing atop a mountain myself. The river perfectly reflects camp. Natives are dressed in animal skins that are thin...They have long hair and about twenty horses. There is a buffalo and dogs. Dead venison and rams are near the right side of my mountain.

We can see how Rick has approached this assignment methodically, starting at the top with the sky and mountains then moving downward to describe the painting's foreground. But I do not feel he has reflected on what he might truly be feeling were he in this scene. It reads instead like a list of what is in the picture.

Martin wrote his postcard while looking at a painting by Martin Johnson Heade entitled *Newbury Port Meadows* (1876), also on view at the Metropolitan's website.

Dear Mama Geeb,

I am here passing by a farm. It's cloudy here in Maine, but there are God's fingers pouring through the clouds. There are little ponds and hay-stacks everywhere. There are even farmers and a horse pulling hay. I wonder how heavy the hay is. I wish you could see these hills. It's a lot better than Brooklyn, (Don't take it personally).

There are piles of dirt in the grass. The grass has so many shades. Green like a frog with a little yellow like a crayon. It is so bright on the ground where it is dark and dreary in the sky. Have you ever seen God's fingers? They are little rays of light that burst through the clouds lighting up the ground. It's really beautiful. Maybe you should come out here and amaze yourself.

Martin.

Martin is not the strongest history student in my class and I enjoyed the opportunity afforded by this assignment to appreciate other aspects of his abilities. His descriptions are vivid and original ("green like a frog") and his use of the term "God's fingers" captures precisely the scene depicted by Heade. I feel that Martin is truly imagining that he is witnessing this scene for himself. His use of the expression, "Don't take it personally" sounds out of place for someone writing in the nineteenth century, but I let that pass. There is a point at which being a stickler does not pay off when it comes to encouraging students to write.

The postcard assignment is an effective writing warm-up exercise for the travelogue. It can also stand on its own as a very short eyewitness assignment. Of course, it can also be pasted into the finished travelogue.

Illustrating the Journey

How can students become genuinely engaged in the past if they cannot imagine it in full color? For this reason I like students to illustrate their travelogues. With practice, students become better equipped to analyze visual documents and thus to learn from them. Nothing focuses a student's attention on the wealth of information contained in a visual document more effectively than using it to sketch from. Students also grow more confident over time in their artistic abilities, especially if you have art teachers at your school who are willing to guide them. Roberto had not been at my school long enough for students to know him well. His exquisite drawings stunned all of us and I made sure to give him plenty of public recognition. Indeed, you may have some students who struggle academically but who are terrific artists; this can be their opportunity to shine.

I first incorporated illustrations in a travelogue assignment while teaching the westward movement using Kathryn Lasky's beautifully written young adult novel *Beyond the Divide* (1983). In it a father and daughter journey west with the hopes of finding gold in California. The young girl is an artist and many of the descriptions in the book focus on her visual appreciation of what she sees. I ask students to imagine themselves as another character on the same wagon train. As we read the book students incorporate details from it into their travelogues and illustrate the journey along the way. If in the novel a wagon wheel breaks, I post a picture of a Conestoga wagon for students to look at. If they encountered a Sioux Indian, I provide students with a picture of Sioux dress. Based on these visual sources (primary sources whenever possible) students create their own artwork. If your students are reluctant to draw, then let them download images they find on the Web to illustrate their journeys. In the end they will have a travelogue that is both informative as well as visually arresting, and they will be doubly proud of the final product.

Reading and Responding to Student Travelogues

Students in my class described themselves in a variety of roles as travelers. Mary wrote:

> My name is Mr. Henry Landon. I am a well-known writer back in England who is deeply respected by the community. Right now I am on a boat headed to the United States and I am nearing my destination, New York City. I have been commissioned to write a book about the United Sates specifically focusing on the three main regions the North, South, and West.

Keith began:

> I am a naturalist. While other people seek ways to develop my beloved

America into a thing of industry and machines I seek to document its beauty and to the best of my ability preserve it.

Erin wrote:

> My journey has started! It will be important for me to write in this old book every night, for someday I will be famous. I will be a well-known actor...With me travels Emma, Lila, and George. With us we carry torn books full of Shakespeare's rhymes, and Victor Hugo's ever so favored poetry.

All of these make good beginnings that introduce us to narrators we will be eager to follow on their journeys. However, good openings do not always lead to the best results. The least successful travelogues were ones that did not incorporate enough factual information. These students wrote from memory without systematically reviewing what they read in their textbooks or what we discussed in class. Their descriptions were vague rather than specific.

Julia, writing as a Londoner, comments on New Orleans:

> We just arrived in New Orleans. We picked up sugar, rice crops, cotton from further up the river, and many other products because New Orleans is a center for preparation, storage, shipping and financing of these things. New Orleans looks very different from Independence, and Joplin. It looks more like London because it is a city. It doesn't look a lot like London just more then it does Independence and Joplin...We are staying just next to a big field of wheat which is perfect for us to get food in. The wheat field is very prosperous.

Julia shows that she does know something about why New Orleans was important as a center of trade. She seems to struggle as she compares it to other cities because she can't imagine them. She would need to look at pictures or get statistics to get a better grasp of what made these cities similar and different. Her comment about staying in a wheat field is troubling. Does she think travelers could just eat the wheat, or does she mean there is a community built up around the wheat field that would feed them? Both her factual understanding and ability to express what she understands seem to be lacking.

On reflection after I first assigned travelogues, I decided that more scaffolding of the assignment would have improved the work of some students, with checklists of precisely what information from what sources to include. On the other hand, the students who were able to work independently really enjoyed the chance to do original research and I often learned a thing or two from them.

For example, Jacob wrote:

> Currently I am in St. Louis, about three months after my visit to New York City. It took very long to go down the Coastal Post Road, across the Wilderness Road, and then down the Mississippi River to Missouri. It is very beautiful here, although quite small compared to New York. Many people are cleaning up what looks like the remainders of a really large fire that burnt down part of the city. When I first arrived in the harbor after my trip from New York, the docks were also wrecked. "There was a huge fire here a month ago," said a local, "A steamboat overheated and blew up, causing a chain-reaction of explosions among the boats, until the city lit on fire."

When I fact-checked this information I found that indeed Jacob was right about it; the fire had taken place in 1849. A little-known fact like this enlivens history.

I ask students to reflect in their conclusions on what they learned about America during the time period.

Mary wrote the following:

> My time spent in the United States has shown me that it is no longer a totally agricultural based country. There is now much manufacturing going on. I am worried that soon its advancements in technology will be ahead of England. I am sure that soon the empty land will become very built up because I definitely see a future in this place. It is quite amazing how I was able to go from the North to the West to the South so fast. I found the three places to be very different. The North is starting to manufacture since Britain's laws no longer forbid it. The middle and southern states are

prospering because their land can be used to plant vital crops. Now that there are faster more efficient ways the crops can be transferred from one region to another the economy is booming.

In this passage Mary demonstrates original insight on several counts. She remains in persona as an English traveler and sees a potential rival in a thriving United States. Her comment that Britain no longer forbids the U.S. to manufacture is not clearly written but I know what she means—before the Revolution England had intentionally squelched the colonies' industrial potential. She understands that as the United States acquires new land its potential will grow, and that despite growing disparity in lifestyles in different regions of the country, technology ("more efficient ways") will help to unite an expanding country. This final paragraph concluded a detailed and vivid account of her travels and let me see that she is able to synthesize what she has learned. She earned high marks on the rubric for this assignment (see end of this chapter).

Using Travelogues as Springboards to Interactive Role-Plays

When implementing a travelogue assignment I like to ensure that students will use what they have learned in an engaging and interactive format. My thinking goes like this: Here we have all these travelers traversing America at a particular time in history. How are we going to put the picture back together?

Congressional Hearings

One format that works well is to find a controversial issue and then hold a congressional hearing about it. The people called to testify are the travelers who have garnered eyewitness information on their journeys. A number of students can role-play members of a congressional committee while other class members role-play the travelers who present their testimony. Here are a few topics worthy of decision-making based on such a congressional investigation:

- What role should Congress and the Federal government play in funding internal improvements (roads, canals, and railways) across the nation? This was a major issue in dispute in the late 1820s and early 1830s with many arguing that it should be the states and not Congress that foot the bill. What regions of the country are in the greatest need of roads, railways, and canals? What influence have existing ones had in terms of the growth of cities and transportation of goods? How fragmented will the nation become without a transportation system to unify it?

- What are the conditions of various native populations and how they are faring under removal policies and enforced schooling? A travelogue assignment that follows the route of explorers west or sojourners to the Gold Rush in California could be the occasion for a congressional hearing addressing these questions.

- During the Great Depression, what types of public works should Congress support, and where? Students can report to Congress on the impact of the Depression in different areas of the country, and the congressional committee can figure out what regional projects the government should fund.

- How should the federal government protect the environment and workers' rights? A congressional hearing for a travelogue set in the Progressive Era or the 1950s could focus on environmental protection and worker's rights around the country.

World's Fair Planning Committee

Another way to integrate what students have learned by completing their travelogues is to hold a meeting of a planning committee for the 1876 Centennial Exhibition held in Philadelphia, the 1893 World's Columbian Exposition held in Chicago, or the 1939 World's Fair held in New York City. Based on travelers' accounts, what exhibitions would the planning committee create to represent different regions of the United States, their people, and their achievements? After proposing their own exhibitions, students can compare them to what was actually featured in the halls of the these events.

Celebration of Regional Cooking

A festive way to end a travelogue assignment is to celebrate America's past with a feast of regional cooking. Students can make family recipes or research and cook dishes that represent ethnic recipes brought by immigrants, the influence of Mexican and native foods in the Southwest, or Southern and African American food traditions.

Assessment

The eyewitness travelogue assignment works best to teach geography and social history, rather than the chronology of historical events. In terms of the thematic strands of the standards developed by the National Council for the Social Studies, the travelogue best enhances students' understanding of Culture (I); People, Places, and Environments (III); Production, Distribution, and Consumption (VII); and Science, Technology, and Society (VIII).

The travelogue provides a portrait of a time period that helps students investigate a number of important issues in American history. These include how social classes and ethnic groups fared at a particular moment in time in different regions of the country; how trade, travel, and technology influenced the unity of the country or further aggravated differences; and how settlement and industrial development affected native peoples and the environment. These are the kinds of issues best addressed by the travelogue assignment.

Rubric for the Travelogue

Topic	Criteria	Mark from 1–5
Writing, Technical	Spelling, grammar, punctuation, syntax, proofreading	
Writing, Artistic	Do you write in the first-person, present tense? Do you provide vivid factual details? Do you provide sensory descriptions (sights, sounds, smells)? Is the vocabulary rich and varied?	
Cities and Sights Along the Way	Do you cover the topics specified by the assignment? Do you incorporate material learned from the text and independent research? Is it relevant and historically accurate?	
Transportation	Do you convey factual material about each mode of transportation? Do you describe its advantages and disadvantages?	
Artwork	Does the artwork reveal effort? Does it reflect historical accuracy? Is it artistically pleasing?	
Conclusion	Do you reflect on what you have seen on your journey? Do you contrast life in different regions of the country? Do you make predictions about the future of the country based on what you have seen?	

Chapter Four

Letters: Arguing the Past in Written Correspondence

The letter you write, whether you realize it or not, is always a mirror which reflects your appearance, taste and character.

Emily Post, 1922

Emailing, instant messaging, and blogging are far from the days of quill pens and ink, yet they have revived the importance of written correspondence in our personal lives. In one fashion or another most students with access to technology know how vital it can feel to be in constant communication with people both near and far. These technologies have also become an important way to sway everyone, from our representatives in Congress to the public at large, in favor of our personal political views.

Reading and analyzing the written correspondence of famous individuals plays an important role in the historian's task of understanding and interpreting history. The letters of common folk also provide crucial insights into history for a "from the bottom up" view of history rather than a "top down" view. Family letters preserved in the attic are valuable because they document the lives and thoughts of people who would otherwise remain voiceless—the soldiers in the trenches rather than the generals, women in their homes rather than men at their desks. Students need to learn how to read and analyze letters as primary source documents (now available extensively on the Web) in order to gain insight into history. These real-life examples serve as models for the writing of their own letters to one another in this eyewitness strategy.

In a letter exchange students are put into pairs and write each other a series of letters. Unlike the pages of so many writing exercises that go from student to teacher, these correspondences give students the pleasure and excitement of both writing and receiving letters. Before letters are written and exchanged, students, working in pairs, imagine who they are and why they are corresponding. From there much of what they write is historical fiction in which they incorporate factual material from their textbooks as well as information about the time period gleaned from primary sources. A sequence of four rounds of letters works well, with a letter written by each student during each round. But a letter exchange is endlessly flexible and lends itself to a variety of models.

My goal in a letter exchange is to have students represent diverse perspectives of the same historical events. By asking students to recount these events as well as the commonplace details of their imaginary lives, I hope to provide them with a visceral understanding of ways in which political events affected people in the past. Today's debates on reforming Social Security will make boring reading in textbooks of the future, but if it is *your* Medicaid benefit or tax hike we are talking about it matters passionately *to you*.

Examining Family Letters

One way to generate excitement for a letter exchange is to ask students to bring to class family letters that have been preserved over one or more generations. My parents have a hatbox in which they have kept all sorts of letters that my grandparents wrote to one another as well as letters that my father sent to my mother during World War II while he was in the U.S. Navy. Even the hatbox is an artifact of the past, and I love bringing it to class. Who wears the types of hats that were kept in hatboxes anymore? The feel of an old letter in the hand is an experience that cannot be duplicated by looking at digitized images, wonderful as those images are. When I assign a letter exchange, I like to say to students, "I want the letters you write to look so authentic and to be so historically accurate that a historian might mistake them for 'the real McCoy.'"

Ideally, your students will have such heirlooms to share in class. Even an envelope can be a source of interesting information. If you gather a bundle of old envelopes together and distribute them to pairs of students they can answer the following questions just by looking at them, or in some cases by doing further research. This kind of exercise is a good introduction to document analysis.

Question to Ask About Old Envelopes

- What does the stamp look like and how much did it cost?
- What does the image on the stamp tell us about heroes of the time period? Are these people we still admire?
- Was the letter mailed before zip codes came into existence? Why were zip codes eventually necessary?
- What kind of seal did the post office use to stamp the letter? Looking at the seal, when was the letter sent? From what U.S. post office was it mailed?
- If the letter has a return address, who sent it and where did he or she live?
- To whom was the letter sent? Where was the recipient living? Do the sender and recipient share a last name?
- What distance did the letter travel? Given the time period, what was the likely means of transportation used to carry the letter?

Looking at the care with which older generations mastered the art of handwriting can lead to an interesting discussion of why handwriting mattered more then than now. And even typewritten letters look quaint these days, with the uneven quality of the ink on the page and the essentially universal font. If no one in the class has family letters to share, local historical societies will often welcome students to view their collections.

Choosing a Time Frame for the Letter Exchange

One of my favorite time periods to study in a letter exchange is the Age of Jackson, during which the nation divided into sectional allegiances. Another is the time period leading up to the Civil War, with letters written about the Kansas Nebraska Act (1854), Bleeding Kansas (1855), the Dred Scott decision (1857), and the Lincoln-Douglas debates (1858). During both of these eras, Americans were increasingly at odds with one another, living very different lifestyles and holding different views in the North and South or out West and in the industrial cities of the East. We can identify with some of the increasing cultural and political discomfort experienced by Americans in the nineteenth century when we think about our own differences as expressed in the categorizations of Red States and Blue States or the supposed East Coast and West Coast outlook versus that of Middle America.

Another way to incorporate differing viewpoints into the letter exchange is to set during wartime—the Revolution, Civil War, World War II, or the Vietnam War, for example. Students are then paired so that one is writing from the battlefront while the other recounts life on the home front.

Before I start a letter exchange I want to convey to students some of the issues that divided Americans during the time period we are studying. Textbook reading is ideal for this kind of background information. It also helps me formulate what roles students can play as correspondents. For example, for a letter exchange set in the late 1820s to mid-1830s, I ask students to read a chapter that is often entitled "Sectional Conflicts" or "Growing Sectionalism" in most U.S. textbooks. From there I begin to make lists of the kinds of people who inhabited each region and the views they may have held on important issues: manufacturers, factory workers, Irish immigrants, bankers, and merchants in the growing industrial North; the aristocratic Southern planters, slaves, and vast numbers of small nonslaveholding farmers in the South; the flood of people of all backgrounds moving West, who will develop a greater allegiance to the nation as a whole than to their region, and the native peoples at whose expense this western migration takes place. I imagine how each group would have experienced the events of the 1830s: a Northern manufacturer is in favor of high tariffs so that his products will not have to compete with lower-priced foreign goods; a Southern planter wants to buy manufactured goods as cheaply as possible and therefore hates the tariff; the Westerner wants roads built at the nation's expense whereas Southerners, bound to their plantations and eager to protect the sovereignty of their states, are opposed to this spending. These are rather dry and abstract issues in the textbook, but a letter exchange will bring them to life. After I choose the time frame, I make every effort to decorate the classroom with images from the time period. Students need to see how people looked, what they wore, their housing, the modes of transportation they used, and so forth.

Partnering Students and Creating Personas

After deciding what issues the letter exchange will address, I partner students into correspondents who will, because of where they live, hold opposing viewpoints on a number of issues. Therefore, one stipulation I make at the start is that each pair must include partners who live in different regions of the country, and we discuss who they might have been. Students must decide on their own what roles they will play (e.g., banker, free person of color moving West, or homemaker renting rooms to boarders, etc.), how they know one another, and why they want to stay connected through letters—their only means of long-distance communication at this time in history.

This leaves open many possibilities for students to formulate their names, their relationship to one another, and where each one lives. Possibilities include a Southern planter writing to a former college roommate at Harvard; a female factory worker in the Lowell Mills of Massachusetts writing to a sister whose family has moved West in search of a better life; a father in the South writing to a son who has moved West as a land speculator; and a free person of color living in the South writing to a relative who has moved North.

Students find it fun to make up their addresses. Because my school is in the historic section of Greenwich Village, many of my students love to imagine themselves living in the 1830 townhouses that still stand. In fact, a few students actually do live in such homes, but they have never thought much about the lives of their predecessors who lived in them. Vanessa lived in an old townhouse, and the letter exchange assignment prompted her to ask her parents what they knew about its history. Who lived there before her family did? How did people cope before plumbing? How could she find out more? Students moving West often wonder whether Indiana or Ohio were states or territories in 1830—a great "teachable moment" for motivating student research. What was the address of a plantation? Questions like these arise when students are trying to develop their "real-life" personas. After partners have formulated their names, relationship to one another, and their addresses, I ask them to fill these in on a chart (see below) that I save so I can keep track of their work.

Students' Names	Imaginary Name	Relationship Between the Correspondents	Fictional Address	Livelihood, Age, and Family Members
Partner 1				
Partner 2				

Next I ask students to write a short biography of themselves up to the date when the letter exchange begins to make their personas more real—much as an actor will flesh out the details of his or her character before making an entrance on the stage. I ask students to answer the following questions and incorporate the answers into a one- or two-page biography. If you prefer, students can simply answer them as they would a questionnaire.

Biography Questionnaire

- What is your age?
- Describe your home and the area in which you live.
- Who are the most important members of your family? Describe them and their relationships to you.
- What was one hardship you faced while growing up?
- Describe the skills you have and the extent of your education.
- What is one accomplishment of which you are proud?

- Describe how you and your family currently supports itself.
- Describe your fears and hopes for the future for yourself and other members of your family.

It is important that writing partners are familiar with one anothers' biographies so that they feel as if they are writing to a real person and respond accordingly. It is also fun, before the letter writing begins, to share the entire cast of characters with the class either by posting their questionnaires or biographies on the bulletin board or by calling up pairs to introduce themselves to the class.

In my experience it is best to partner students of approximately equal ability, especially in terms of their writing skills. Although it is true that an accomplished student writer could coach and inspire a weaker writer, I usually find that my most motivated students get frustrated if they write their hearts out only to receive a short and poorly written response. And what happens if your class has an odd instead of even number of students? It is possible to create trios (a mother and father writing to a daughter, for example). Another possibility is for you to partner with a student and become a letter writer yourself!

Students become more invested in their imaginary personas when they go in search of a portrait to match their biography. In any letter exchange set in the period after the discovery of daguerreotypes (1839), students can use old photographs. It is lots of fun to find discarded portraits at flea markets, and I have enjoyed gathering a collection of my own that students can photocopy. Daguerreotypes can also be downloaded from the Web at American Memory's collection, "America's First Look into the Camera: 1839–1862." By studying these photographs students will acquire a feeling for how people looked, dressed, and deported themselves during the time period. You can make this activity even more fun by asking your technology department to help students use an image-editing program such as Fireworks, which enables students to cut and paste photos of their faces onto old portraits! Students can create sketches of themselves for a letter exchange set before the 1840s, and old magazines (as well as the Internet) can be a great source of photographs from more recent times.

The Letter Assignments

A letter exchange should have a minimum of two rounds of letters — each student writes one letter, receives one letter to which they respond, and then receives a second one. This is what makes a letter exchange interactive. I like to include four rounds in order to cover a greater amount of historical material, but I speed the process up by having each round of letters written simultaneously (no one waits for a first letter respond to respond to; they all just start in). In effect, student letters cross in the mail. I play the role of the postman, gathering all their letters in a pouch and distributing them to the addressees—always a dramatic moment. Maggie and Christina were best friends who were notorious gossips, lingering in hallways to chat, arriving late to class, passing notes, and so forth. But they were both excellent writers, so I decided to take a chance and pair them as correspondents. They became so engrossed in the life and times of the characters they created that they could not wait to get to class to open the latest letters they had written to one another.

I insist that each letter in an exchange includes several components. In every letter students express their viewpoints about one historical event and describe ongoing developments in their personal lives. In each letter they must also discuss a cultural activity (such as a book they have read or a play they attended) or relate their thoughts or experiences concerning a scientific or technological advance (such as a recent invention they used or a medical treatment). In addition, they must enclose with each letter something tangible but small, such as a portrait, sketch, news clipping, or keepsake. The enclosures allow creative and artistic students to put their multiple intelligences to work in order to bring the time period to life. David was not noteworthy as a diligent student, but he was a gifted artist, something his classmates were not aware of. So I made a point of holding up his artistic and detailed sketches so the class could "Ooh" and "Ah" a bit. These components of a letter exchange work to bring the whole period to life and to contextualize both personal and political events. A wonderful reference book for both teacher and students to use is *The Timetables of American History* edited by Laurence Urdang (2001). For each year in U.S. history this book lists important events both in America and elsewhere under the headings "History and Politics," "The Arts," and "Science & Technology."

The following grid explains the assignments I made for an Age of Jackson letter exchange. The overriding issues here center on the expansion of democracy and the use of power—Jackson's ousting of the New England and Virginia aristocrats from power and his own sometimes overreaching use of power (in supporting Cherokee Removal despite a Supreme Court ruling, for example). I found that once I established the basic assignment it was easy to change and refocus the assignment each year depending upon the sophistication of the class, their interests and mine, and just where I wanted to leave off and begin. You can add more political issues for students to discuss. For example, in 1831 students could also be asked to write about Nat Turner's rebellion and the founding of Garrison's *The Liberator*. While it is important for students to comment on political issues in chronological order, I left it to them to decide which cultural or scientific issues they would cover when and what artifacts they would enclose with the letters.

The Rounds of the Letter Exchanges

Round One: 1829

Political	Jackson has been inaugurated president. What is your opinion of him and why? He has initiated the spoils system that kicks office holders of the opposing party out of their positions. Is this a good idea or destructive party politics?
Personal	Describe your ongoing personal life, such as business or farming successes and failures, family life, births, marriages, and deaths, etc.
Cultural or Scientific	Describe an experience with one of the latest modes of transportation (canal boat, steamboat, or railroad).
Enclosure	Enclose a sketch or photograph of your imaginary self.

Round Two: 1830

Political	South Carolina has threatened to secede from the Union in response to the Tariff of Abominations. How has the tariff affected you and your neighbors? Senators Webster and Hayne have just had a debate on states' rights and nullification. What are your views on these issues and why?
Personal	Describe your ongoing personal life, such as business or farming successes and failures, family life, births, marriages, and deaths, etc.
Cultural or Scientific	Describe a cultural event or social gathering such as a concert, play, lecture, or church service.
Enclosure	Enclose a drawing you make such as a map, layout of your home, political cartoon, or advertisement.

Round Three: 1831–1832

Political	The Bank War. President Jackson is firmly opposed to rechartering the national Bank of the United States. Should he veto the new charter? Depending upon where you live and your occupation, how do you feel about this issue? The Supreme Court upholds the rights of the Cherokee Indians. What is your position regarding their removal West?
Personal	Describe your ongoing personal life, such as business or farming successes and failures, family life, births, marriages, and deaths, etc.
Cultural or Scientific	Describe a recent book or publication you have read, such as *The Liberator*, *The Last of the Mohicans*, or *The Emigrant's Best Instructor*.
Enclosure	Enclose a keepsake or small package, such as a lock of hair, pack of seeds, fabric swatch, or legal document.

Round Four: 1832

Political	Andrew Jackson is running for a second term against Henry Clay. Are you a Democrat voting for Jackson or a National Republican voting for Clay? Whom do you favor and why? Disagree strongly with your correspondent and try to persuade him or her of your viewpoint.
Personal	Describe your ongoing personal life, such as business or farming successes and failures, family life, births, marriages, and deaths, etc.
Cultural or Scientific	Describe an experience involving a new household, business, or farm invention, such as the McCormick reaper or the telegraph.
Enclosure	Enclose a clipping from your local newspaper

Reading Letters as Historical Documents

A letter exchange presents an opportune time to teach students how to write a letter as well as how to analyze letters as historical documents. By looking at a sample correspondence, students can begin to do both. I often use two letters from the collection of family letters in Robert Manson Myers's book *The Children of Pride: A True Story of Georgia and the Civil War* (1984). The first letter in the collection was written in 1860 by Charles C. Jones Jr., the newly-elected mayor of Savannah, to his father the Reverend C. C. Jones, a prominent Presbyterian minister in Montevideo, Georgia.

Hon. Charles C. Jones, Jr., to Rev. and Mrs. C. C. Jones

Savannah, Wednesday, November 7th, 1860
My dear Father and Mother,
    We are happy today to hear from you so directly. Mr. Buttolph came in while we were at dinner and gave us the latest news from you. The watch and spectacles are already in the hands of the jeweler, and will be repaired so soon as practicable. You shall have them by the earliest opportunity thereafter. The volume is now in charge of the express company, and will be duly forwarded to Mr. _____. In consideration of

the fact of my being His Honor the Mayor, the agent refused to receive any pay for the transportation of the same.

The telegrams announce the fact of Lincoln's election by a popular vote! South Carolina has today virtually seceded. Judge Magrath of the U.S. Circuit Court for the District of South Carolina, Hon. William F. Colcock, collector of the port of Charleston, and other government officers have resigned, and we learn that the Palmetto flag will be hoisted on the morrow. A meeting of the citizens here is called for tomorrow evening. We are on the verge of Heaven only knows what.

I write in haste for the mail. You have my congratulations, Father, upon the near completion of your first volume. May you have increasing mind and strength to conclude your most valuable labors! Ruth will, my dear mother, be very happy to get the turkeys at some convenient and early day. Our little Julia is recovering from her attack of broken-bone fever, but my dear Ruth is quite unwell, and has been suffering much for nearly a week. They unite with me, my dear parents, in warmest love to you both. As ever,

> Your affectionate son,
> Charles C. Jones, Jr.

Rev. C. C. Jones to Hon. Charles C. Jones, Jr.

Montevideo [Georgia], Monday, November 19th, 1860
My dear Son,

I shall send, D. V., our shoe measure tomorrow to Messrs. Butler & Frierson to fit and forward by Friday's freight train. Will you do me the favor of calling and selecting the quality and price for me? The first I wish substantial, the second not extravagant. Have notified them that you would do so.

Your sister reached us in safety, and improved by her pleasant visit to you. The little one's pretty well, and very engaging. We want Ruthie and little Julia to come and see us. The change will do them good, and we will do all in our power to make it agreeable in our quiet home.

Preached yesterday at Midway, and do not feel the worse for it today.

Tomorrow the county holds a meeting on Federal affairs... Shall attend, Providence permitting; and Mother says she will go with me to represent her father, being the oldest child of his family now living. You know her patriotism. She has taken possession of your pistol with the shooting apparatus underneath, and Gilbert is ordered to clean and put it in perfect order. And she says she has caps for it. I trust the measure of the state will be calmly considered and resolutely taken, and the convention of the people duly called.

Mother and Sister unite with me in love to Ruthie and yourself, and kisses for Julia. I am longing to see the child...

    Your affectionate father,

      C.C. Jones

One of the first things to consider when analyzing letters, as historian Steven Stowe (2002) reminds us, is that "Letters are shaped by the contingencies of distance and time between writer and recipient; they become over time scattered in various places and must be 'collected' to form a single body of writing." Stowe points out that when looking at collections it is helpful to remember that, "Letters tend to cluster around certain key events: births, separations over time and distance, sickness and health, courtships and marriages, and deaths." (Stowe's thought-provoking essay, "Making Sense of Letters and Diaries," and sample exercises for analyzing historical letters can be found on the History Matters website.)

Before students read the body of a letter they can analyze a great deal by noting when the letter was written, the relationship between the writer and recipient, where each resides, and the terms of address used in the opening and closing of the letter. Already they are in possession of important information that will make reading the letter seem less daunting. How do these pieces of information help us read the letter itself? First students can draw on their prior knowledge about what life was like in 1860. In turn they can make deductions about the time period from details in the letter. The overriding events of 1860 are Lincoln's election and the secession of South Carolina, both referred to in the first letter. We can deduce that the various meetings alluded to by father and son are convening in order to decide whether or not Georgia will follow South Carolina's lead and secede

("Tomorrow the county holds a meeting on Federal affairs").

Even if students do not understand every word in the letters, they can deduce a good deal simply by listing the words they find that describe the material culture and technology in the 1860s. The letter writers refer to watches, spectacles, a gun, the express company, telegrams and freight trains. The correspondents do not yet know that war will break out ("We are on the verge of Heaven only knows what"), but we know with hindsight that the telegraph and railroads will be key players in the coming war. In the midst of events that will shake the very foundations of their world, father and son are also concerned with very routine matters—the ordering of shoes, for example. Students can pick up the strong feelings for family ties even if they do not figure out precise relationships (sister, grandchildren, and so forth).

The very formal salutations and closings tell us something about social mores at this time in history. Stowe (2002) points out that whether written for a professional or personal audience, letter writers express themselves within the conventions of their day, and one's letter was often judged by how well it measured up to epistolary models. The formality of the name and the use of the term "affectionate" in the closing phrase "Your affectionate son, Charles C. Jones, Jr." may strike us as oxymoronic, but at the time it was simply considered proper form.

We can also learn a good deal about gender roles from letters such as these. Mrs. Jones attends a political meeting but feels she must justify her attendance there by claiming that she is representing her father. She then takes it upon herself to see that her son's gun is cleaned. Her husband writes, "You know her patriotism." Can we figure out from these letters whether the members of the family are secessionists or unionists? What does "patriotism" mean in the midst of a country torn in two? What questions do these letters raise that others in the collection may answer?

We can see, then, that the Jones letters provide students with models for writing their own. They interweave the personal with the political, and they convey the technological and sociological realities of their day. We can also see the ways in which personal items are being sent between the recipients for practical reasons (a volume of the father's book, jewelry, shoes). It also pays to remember that in the days when a letter was the *only* connection possible between two people separated by distance, "The physical object [of the letter] itself came to represent the absent person's touch and nearness" (Stowe 2002). For this reason, Stowe goes on to point out, Americans cherished letters as objects, preserving them in private places.

Writing Letters as a Necessary Skill

A letter exchange provides the English or social studies teacher with an opportunity to teach letter writing form—the placement of addresses and date, what terms of address to use with whom, appropriate salutations and closings, and what punctuation and capitalization to use. When these skills are taught out of context they are not much fun to learn, but they can be fun when put to use and given meaning by the context of a letter exchange.

I recommend using old etiquette manuals to teach these skills. Studying letter writing of the past as well as the present will enable students to become more astute readers of historical correspondence, help them to make their letters sound authentic, and also teach them basic skills. An inveterate collector at rummage sales, I happened to pick up an etiquette manual many years ago entitled *The Ladies and Gentlemen's Etiquette: A Complete Manual of the Manners and Dress of American Society Containing Forms of Letters, Invitations, Acceptances and Regrets With a Copious Index*, by Mrs. E. B. Duffey, published in 1877. The book is fascinating for what it reveals about gender roles and social class, and a few excerpts from a guide such as this one are worth discussing in class. The author says that as to a family letter:

> *Women always write these best. They know how to pick up those little items of interest which are, after all, nearly the sum-total of home life, and which, by being carefully narrated, transport, for the time being, the recipient back to home and interests…Having furnished all the news, they should make kind and careful inquiries concerning the feelings and doings of the recipient; and if this recipient is not an adept in the art of letter-writing, they may furnish questions enough to be answered to make the reply an easy task. They should conclude with sincere expressions of affection from all the members of the family to the absent one, a desire for his speedy return or best welfare, and a request for an early answer. (111–112)*

You can point out to students how E. B. Duffey models for her readers the taste for flowery and convoluted sentences so admired in the nineteenth century. Students will profit from her practical advice when they respond to the letter they have just received. Duffey advises the letter writer to respond to questions asked and pose others; doing so will ensure that the student pair exchange different viewpoints on a variety of issues.

Another excerpt from an etiquette book worthy of discussion with students is this introduction to the chapter titled "Longer Letters" in Emily Post's 1922 etiquette book, available online at Bartleby.com.

> *The art of general letter-writing in the present day is shrinking until the letter threatens to become a telegram, a telephone message, a post-card. Since the events of the day are transmitted in newspapers with far greater accuracy, detail, and dispatch than they could be by the single effort of even Voltaire himself, the circulation of general news, which formed the chief reason for letters of the stage-coach and sailing-vessel days, has no part in the correspondence of to-day.*

Discuss with students the means of communication available to people then and now. Why has the telegraph all but disappeared while the postcard remains with us? How do email and instant messaging affect not only what people write, but the words, spelling, and sentence structures they choose? How is Emily Post's advice from 1922 still applicable? In what ways does it sound antiquated?

Student Letters

For the Age of Jackson letter exchange, Corrine wrote as Edward Pickering, a New York banker residing at 140 Broadway in New York City writing to his cousin, Wilbur Pickering (Jesse) who has moved West with his family and is living in Hicksville, Tennessee. I have underlined their references to the things they enclosed with their letters.

New York City, June 10, 1829
Dearest Cousin Wilbur,
I am truly sorry for my belated letter. My wife and children are do-

ing fine, actually wonderful. How about your family? I hope all is well. My children are definitely growing up. Elizabeth is already engaged to a sophisticated, well-educated and charming young man...

Congratulations again on Ann *[who just had a baby]*. You must be so proud. Victoria is expecting a child this fall and all the family is excited...Remember Harry Butterworth, our neighbor? I believe you met him several times. Anyway, he passed away. The family is all upset. He was part of our family. However, Harry was quite elderly, so he had a very full life, in my opinion. I enclosed the obituary because it is quite sweet. The whole idea has saddened me and I have not been able to function that well. I hope that mother is well. We are going to visit her, on the estate, in two weeks time. It is quite a lengthy trip from New York to Albany and so we will probably take the awful railway car because it will be much faster than a steamboat...

I am horrified that Jackson has won the election. I am dreadfully sorry if that offended you but I believe that Jackson will take the progressing country and turn it completely upside down. Jackson's system of "spoils" is a ridiculous one. Just because he is the president doesn't mean that he can throw out any federal worker who was working for the Whigs. I know it does not affect you in the least bit, but one of my closest friends, Thomas Elderidge, was thrown out of his position in the government. He lives in Washington, D.C. and he went to the Inauguration of Jackson to hear Jackson speak and to see the people's reaction. This is how he described it to me: "There were so many people. All the carriages, horses, donkeys, caravans were scattered in the area. The noise was unbearable and I could barely hear what the president was saying. I found a completely chaotic scene but a spirit and bond between all the people for Jackson..."

You see, Jackson should not be the one who is now being honored at an inauguration. It should have been Adams...

I am reading a book called The Dutchman's Fireside by Paulding. It is about life in upstate New York during the French and Indian war.

I hope you are enjoying the spring weather and that your family is well. Send me a letter soon with news.

Fondly, Your Cousin Edward Pickering

January 10, 1830

Hicksville, Tennessee

Dear Edward,

Congratulations! I am thrilled to hear about Victoria's pregnancy. Just think, another niece or nephew that I can bounce upon my knee until they grow-up and get married just like Elizabeth soon will.

Do you know what just happened to me? Well, last month I wanted to get a loan from the National Bank so I could expand and buy more property for my farming. Well, they turned me down when I have perfectly good collateral. They said, "Sorry, You're too much of a risk for us to invest in." Risk? Humph! They took a risk not investing in me. The nerve of some people! The only reason they wouldn't loan to me was because I am from Hicksville, Tennessee. It's a good thing Jackson is throwing out of office the Eastern snobs who have not a clue what it is needed by hard working Americans like me. This is the exact reason why I approve of Jackson vetoing the National Bank. There's nothing national about it. They should rename it "only loan to the rich" bank. The bank is totally biased and unfair. I will be happy when it's gone…I also approve of Jackson's strong stand on the removal of the Indians west. He wants this for the good of the whole nation. No more midnight massacres (my friend was almost killed in an Indian raid out west) no more keeping good soil, land and gold to themselves. I always said Jackson was the better man and I will vote for him again.

Edward, what I am about to write is strictly confidential, not even Sue-Ann knows this, but I might lose the farm! You're the last person I can turn to for help. I haven't got enough money to pay the mortgage and keep a family alive, so I'm asking, begging you, my favorite cousin to help me out of a jam. (Remember all those summers when I covered for you?) I know you are just getting the bank back together, but you're my last resort. Don't worry, I'll pay you back. I am an honest man. Please, help me.

Well, now that I got that out of the way I just want to mention that Cora Ann lost her first tooth. Sue-Ann and I are so proud of our little genius. (Enclosed is her tooth and picture, you should love it.)

Your Eternally faithful, Cousin Wilbur

We can see from these letters that Corrine and Jesse have created characters that seem to live and breathe. The story evolves as they write to each other. Cousin Wilbur asks Edward for a loan to demonstrate the economic straits he is in and to show that the National Bank is of little use to those out West, far from the well-connected people of the East Coast. This in turn creates a twist in the plot they will need to solve in the next set of letters: Will Edward loan his cousin money? What will happen to their relationship and Wilbur's finances if Edward refuses the loan?

In Wilbur's letter we see ideas expressed about the removal of the Indians from their homelands by the federal government. Jesse, like all my students, condemned the removal of Indians from their homelands, but in the character of Wilbur he expressed a desire to get rid of them. Although some Americans condemned their removal at the time, most either agreed with Jesse's persona or were silent about it. It is much easier to condemn injustice when your own interests are not at stake, and it is important for students to understand that the mind-set of people living in the past allowed such injustice to happen. As they argue about political events from their personal viewpoints they are reinforcing their knowledge of history and understanding it on a deeper level than they would if they had merely memorized dry facts.

Edward enclosed an obituary with this letter, a small typed column supposedly clipped from a newspaper but actually one that Corrine had written. Jesse (writing as Wilbur) included a baby tooth. I find that students have enormous fun creating the enclosures, and I have seen a great variety of them—drawings of homesteads, maps of their towns, pieces of calico fabric, advertisements for miracle medicines, and programs from concerts. The enclosures make the letters exciting to open and, when posted on the bulletin board with the letters, make for a visually arresting display.

We can see also that students are using a variety of primary and secondary sources as they write, including their textbooks. The description of Jackson's inauguration was based on a primary source the class read, a letter written by Margaret Bayard Smith on March 11, 1829, from Washington D.C. It is available in many anthologies as well as on the Web. The railway journey described by Edward gives me an opportunity to encourage students to do more research: Did Corrine look at a map? Did such a route exist? And would the train at this date have been faster than a steamboat?

Evaluating Students' Letters

There are a variety of ways to respond to students' letters. I always want to find out how students are approaching an assignment like this one early on so that I can get them on track as the activity continues. For this reason I want to be certain to give students feedback on their first round of letters. Because I want their letters to remain authentic-looking, I never write directly on them unless I want a student to rewrite one. Correcting spelling is one thing I forego on this assignment, because in truth, our ancestors did not spell perfectly either. At this point I am looking to see if the students are following directions, incorporating factual material into their letters, and inventing a plausible plot. Sometimes students get carried away or take the opportunity to become silly; the address of "Hicksville, Tennessee" is an example. As I respond to the first letters, I keep in mind questions such as, Are they invested in their characters and writing enough to give the assignment justice? Are they furthering their knowledge of history? One year two students created characters who wrote to each other about their adulterous affairs. The students were very engaged in this endeavor, but I did not think this was appropriate to the assignment and I asked them to rewrite their letters.

Although I like to fill in a rubric sheet for each letter written, I don't always have the time. In that case I skim all letters in the first round, both to flag work that is not up to par as well as to select a few letters worthy of being read aloud so the class has models to emulate. We discuss how the authors of these models made their characters vivid and how they used factual details to bring the era to life.

In terms of responding to subsequent rounds of correspondence (and you can opt to have just one additional round), there are a variety of strategies I recommend. One is to use a portfolio model in which each student selects one letter from their correspondence to submit for grading. This forces students to reflect on their own letters and cuts down on the time you spend assessing their work. A variation on this approach is to treat each pair like a cooperative learning team—together they must choose their best round of letters to submit knowing that they will each receive the same grade for the sum of what they turn in. This builds incentive to work as a team and a desire to improve one another's work.

Sharing Student Work

There are a variety of valuable ways to share and celebrate student work. First, I encourage correspondents to share their perspectives on events when we discuss them in class. I try to build a climactic end to a letter exchange so that students will be geared up for some heated debates over the issues during class discussions. The topics will vary depending on the time period in which the letter exchange is set. The discussion topic could be on whom to vote for in the upcoming election, whether or not the South should secede from the Union, whether or not the U.S. should withdraw from Vietnam, and so forth. In the case of a home front/ battlefront letter exchange the focus is not on formulating arguments but on sharing perspectives on what life is like during wartime.

Another means of sharing viewpoints is to call students up in pairs for a dramatic reading of their letters. You can ask them to wear costumes and find appropriate props. A staged reading of the letters creates an entertaining event for a wider school audience. If this is too time-consuming you can put students into groups of four or six and ask them to read their letters to one another in small groups.

One thing I would always recommend is that you post the letters on a huge bulletin board with students'

Fig 4.1 A student took time to make this envelope look as if it really was from earlier times.

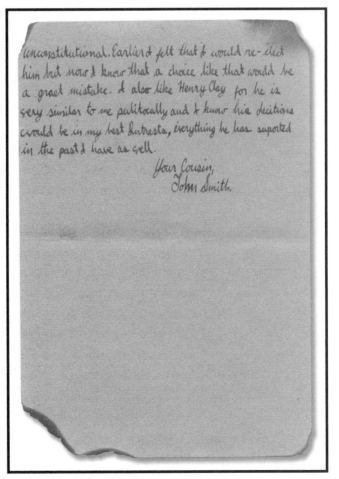

Fig 4.2 In a letter to a "cousin," this student describes an individual's thoughts on the election campaign of Andrew Jackson versus Henry Clay.

real names above and their correspondence below. The enclosures make this a particularly engaging display. To entice students to read all the letters, ask them to cast a vote for any correspondence except their own in categories such as "most engaging storyline," "best use of historical facts," and "best enclosures."

Variations on the Theme of Letter Writing

Covering a Decade

Another useful model for a letter exchange covers more chronological ground. Students begin and end their correspondence in different years, with each consecutive pair taking on a later time period. Thus you can cover the Great Depression and World War II by asking one pair to write about the Stock Market Crash of 1929, the next to write about President Hoover's response, the following pair to write about the election of Roosevelt in 1932, and so forth. Materials for implementing this model are published by Interact and are available for twentieth-century American history.

Answering the Letters of Famous People

For another variation, students can answer or respond to the published letters of famous people. The presidential libraries are wonderful sources of digitized documents. The Eisenhower archives contains letters written to and from the president relating to the Civil Rights movement, McCarthyism, and the Korean War, to name just a few. In one letter, Clyde R. Miller, writing from Columbia University on June 8, 1953, asks President Eisenhower to grant executive clemency to Julius and Ethel Rosenberg in the famous spy case. After your students learn about Eisenhower as a man and a leader, ask them to write Eisenhower's response to Miller's letter. What would he have to say? How would he say it? Compare students' responses to the letter Eisenhower actually wrote—also available online. A good deal about the exigencies of a time period and the character of a president can be elucidated by such an exercise.

Role-Playing Famous Correspondents

An activity such as the one above can be taken a step further if students role-play both partners in a famous correspondence, such as that of John and Abigail Adams. They can read the actual correspondence up to a certain point and then take over from there. Another tack is to ask them to write letters on a topic about which the historical figures are not known to have written to one another, or to imagine what they would write about a hot topic today, such as the debate on the role of religion in our democracy.

Assessment

The letter exchange is an effective way to teach a sequence of important historic events. At the same time, the history we teach students need not be exclusively political and military. Feminist historians, for example, have long emphasized that to understand gender roles and the contributions women have played throughout U.S. history, more attention must be paid to social history. Along with political events, a letter exchange teaches students the ways in which the arts and technology provide individuals with new frameworks for understanding their world, for making money, for traveling, and for providing healthcare and education. By filling in a picture of how people lived in the past, the zeitgeist of the time period takes on life. The interactive partnerships between students enliven the classroom and motivate students to learn from each other. In the meantime, students have learned the real-life skill of how to write letters while beginning to understand the role letters play as primary source documents.

Rubric for a Letter Exchange

Topic	Criteria	Mark from 1–5
Writing, Technical	Do you use correct letter-writing conventions for the time period? Do you use correct grammar, punctuation, and syntax?	
Writing, Artistic	Do you provide vivid and accurate factual details? Do you provide sensory descriptions (sights, sounds, smells)? Is the vocabulary rich, varied, and appropriate to the time period?	
Historical Content	Do you incorporate historical events into your narrative, as per instructions? Do you include facts and relevant detail? Do you react to what your correspondent has written to you? Do you explain your point of view in response to questions or differences of opinion?	
Personal Narrative	Do you create a personal narrative? Do you show how historical events influenced your own life? Is your narrative credible for the time period?	
Enclosures	Do you follow instructions about what to include with each letter? Do your enclosures reflect research about the era? Do your enclosures reflect effort and artistry?	
Teamwork and Class Discussion	Did you work effectively with your partner? Did you contribute regularly to class discussion? Did you effectively represent your viewpoint in class?	
Overall Comment:		

Chapter Five

Newspapers: Conflicting Accounts of the Same Events

Let the people know the facts, and the country will be safe.

Abraham Lincoln, 1864

Students always become engaged when I ask them to write a newspaper set in the historical period under study. Because newspapers are corporate by nature and reflect the coordinated efforts of editors, reporters, and publishers, the newspaper assignment becomes a team effort. Perhaps this is one reason it excites students; they get to work together to create a final product. Unlike letters and diaries, newspapers are written directly *to* the public, ostensibly to inform but often to persuade. This is a public voice, not a private one, and for students it entails learning to write in journalistic style. But although the typical newspaper assignment effectively captures the eyewitness point of view, it fails to take this perspective where it should lead: into conflicting interpretations of the same events.

Whatever period you want to illuminate through a conflicting newspaper assignment, remember that the activity offers an excellent opportunity to teach about the role technology played in both gathering and disseminating the news. How did the introduction of the telegraph, telephone, or video camera change how news was gathered and conveyed to the public? While the teaching strategies presented in this chapter discuss print media, the approach can easily be adapted to other student-created news formats such as radio talk shows or video telecasts.

Newspapers also offer students a chance to study the changing role of American women, both black and white, who had the opportunity to become journalists and photographers. Prominent writers include Margaret Fuller, Lydia Maria Child, and Jane Swisshelm from the antebellum period; muckraker Ida Tarbell; Dorothy Thompson, a newspaper correspondent in the 1930s; and Charlayne Hunter-Gault, a civil rights activist. Journalistic style has changed over time, and eyewitness accounts can reflect these changes as well.

The Revolutionary War and Civil War lend themselves to being seen from conflicting viewpoints within American society, Rebel versus Tory and North versus South. A newpaper's partisanship was overt and often strident during these wars, unlike today when newspapers strive for objectivity. A newspaper assignment set at the turn of the nineteenth century would offer students the chance to learn about the sensationalist press or "yellow journalism" and the beginnings of investigative journalism developed by the muckrakers. The Vietnam War, which so divided Americans in the 1960s and 1970s, is a time period that can be illuminated by prowar and antiwar newspapers. In fact, this period spawned an array of alternative and underground newspapers, such as *The Village Voice*, *The San Francisco Oracle*, and the *East Village Other*, that challenged the veracity of reporting in the establishment press. They were widely distributed. Their journalists developed a freewheeling and personal voice sometimes referred to as "new journalism" that is fun for students to explore in their own writing. Newspapers of this era offered not only opposing interpretations of events, but vastly different styles of presenting the news.

When assigning students to work on newspaper teams, I tell them what side of the conflict they must support, and I divide the class evenly into the viewpoints I want represented. (Sometimes there are more than two, as is discussed later.) How many newspapers get published by each side depends upon how many students I have in a class. Teams should not get so big that they cannot work effectively as a group; five to eight students per team works well. Each team is then assigned to cover the same list of topics, but each must give the news a different slant or spin.

I discovered the effectiveness of assigning conflicting newspapers somewhat by default. One year I had taken too much time on the events leading up to the Civil War, and thus I had to cover the war years themselves in short order. I only had time to assign reading from the textbook, which reduced some of the most exciting years in American history to a dull recitation of the facts, whereas surely Northerners and Southerners had experienced events from very different viewpoints encompassing very different emotions. How could I enliven the textbook account? I decided to ask each student to write one newspaper article for either a Northern or Southern special edition of a newspaper—a retrospective look at all four years of the war—written as if they were living in 1865.

Even in its early, simplest form this assignment transformed students' reading of the text. In *The Story of America* (1991), John A. Garraty writes, "After capturing Atlanta, Sherman burned the city to the ground. The next day, November 15, his army set out eastward toward the city of Savannah on the Atlantic Coast" (583). I asked students to stop and analyze these sentences from different vantage points. Imagine the North's jubilation at "capturing Atlanta" and the despondency of the South as Sherman "burned the city to the ground." And how different each side must have felt as Sherman's army "set out eastward toward the city of Savannah"!

Reading Primary Source News Accounts

In subsequent years the idea of writing newspapers from opposing viewpoints took off and became a major assignment that I built into the curriculum. Whatever the dateline for student newspapers, it is important for students to read contemporaneous primary source documents—the rhetoric of actual news reporting—to capture the flavor of the times and make their own writing sound more authentic. Examples for newspapers from the Civil War are not hard to find. The *Brooklyn Daily Eagle* dating from the 1840s is now online for free. The *New York Times* archives (beginning in 1851) can be accessed through a subscription to ProQuest or directly through the *New York Times* website. Various Southern newspapers have been transcribed at a variety of university websites (see Appendix E). It is interesting for students to contrast the account of the fall of Atlanta in their textbooks to newspaper accounts written at the time. The article "Exiles from Atlanta" from the *Charleston Mercury* of September 27, 1864, captures the author's effort to call attention to the plight of refugees. Today it is reminiscent of accounts of the devastation wrought by hurricane Katrina; then as now we are prompted by such news stories to offer what aid we can. But the tone of the writing is different from what we are used to today, with the author's heart very much on his or her sleeve (there is no byline).

Charleston Mercury, September 27, 1864, p. 1, c. 2

> *The Exiles from Atlanta*
> *The condition of the poor refugees and exiles from Atlanta must be pitiable in the extreme...Just think of it. Almost a thousand children exposed to the inclemency of the weather, and with scarcely food enough to eke out their miserable lives. The Mayor's Office [of Macon, Georgia] is thronged with these unfortunate women daily, who with tears plead merely for bread that their little ones may not starve...Destitute of home, money, food or strong arms to provide these things for them, they present a sickening aspect. Many of them have young babes at the breast...In the name of justice, we beg the people to go to work and mitigate the circumstances of these people. (*Charleston Mercury 1864*)*

Here is how *Harper's Weekly Journal of Civilization*, reporting for the North, reflects on the beginning of the war when it is almost over on March 18, 1865 (see Figure 5.1):

A Visit to Fort Sumter

> *There is a thrilling dramatic effect in the repossession of Fort Sumter four years after its surrender to traitors. Every thing [sic] connected with the capture of Charleston has more or less of this dramatic interest. Here the rebellion had its birth, and after four years of a strife the most terrible as well as the most needless on record, after four years which have done very much toward exhausting the Confederate States, the*

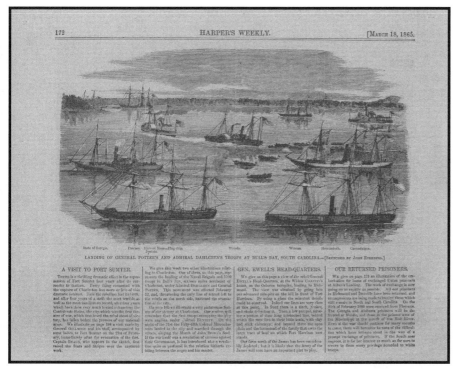

Fig 5.1 Overtly sentimental language was par for the course in the newspapers of the Civil War era.

*city which was the first theatre of war, which first heard the rebel shout of victory, has fallen before the prowess of our national arms. (*Harper's Weekly *1865b)*

When reading such accounts, students are immediately struck by the stark use of the word *traitors* instead of the word we commonly use today, *rebels*. The difference in vantage point, North and South, then and now, influences what words writers choose to describe events. I ask students to consider this when they write their news stories. The article strikes a more emotional tone than we are used to in the news reporting of today, and like the article from the *Charleston Mercury*, its author is not ashamed to play upon our feelings. Nineteenth-century journalists strove for sentimentality, something we try to avoid. I ask students to separate the author's use of facts with which we would all agree ("here the rebellion had its birth"), from value judgments that are debatable ("the most needless [conflict] on record"). The author's use of rhetoric plays on an implied use of opposites: the rebellion's birth with its death, and the "rebel shout of victory" with its implicit defeat.

A Classroom Simulation for Teaching Point of View

I like to teach about the eyewitness perspective by holding a brief simulation in the classroom. This is an activity my high school teacher Carole Losee used in the 1960s, and it made such an impression that I never forgot it. She arranged a staged commotion during class by asking two older students and a fellow teacher to simultaneously barge into the classroom. The teacher argued with Ms. Losee while the students rummaged about looking for lost items and picked fights with other students. We thought it was all happening for real. I was shocked to see mild-mannered Ms. Losee turn red with anger and hear her shout vociferously at the intruders.

When I do this same activity with my classes my students often feel a bit embarrassed to be duped. "You mean you staged the whole thing?" they ask. After the intrusion is over I ask students to write an account of the "historical event." We read aloud what they have written, and we compare their accounts. Invariably no single student is able to capture everything that went on in the same few minutes; what each student experienced varies depending upon where he or she was seated and with whom they interacted. How then to get an accurate depiction of everything that occurred simultaneously? After we discuss the simulation my students agree that historians must wade through the evidence, assessing the reliability of each witness. By noticing which accounts are corroborated by other eyewitnesses, historians can begin to draw conclusions. This simulation makes an important point: just because someone is an eyewitness to an event, it does not mean he or she knows more about it than historians.

Following the simulation, I ask the class to imagine how hard it must be to figure out what happened in the immediate aftermath of a major battle. We discuss how reporters' sympathies for one side or the other might affect how they interpret what they witnessed. A helpful analogy for students is to compare a battle like Antietam to a high school football or basketball match against a rival team; your emotional take on events is very different depending on whether you are the home team or the visiting team. In this hypothetical case no one can dispute who won—the score board tells us—

but how often does the losing side put the blame on an unfair referee rather than on his or her teammates?

Apart from inadvertent bias in news reporting, the deliberate slanting or falsification of the news is often encouraged during wartime, and publication of the whole truth is sometimes prohibited. One justification is that bad news is bad for morale. In "The Southern People Undeceived," which also appeared in the March 18, 1865, issue of *Harper's Weekly*, the author aims to bolster Northern confidence and resolve while attempting to persuade Southerners to jump ship.

The Southern People Undeceived

*Why should the rebel leaders wonder that the people around them no longer trust them? The Southern people are rapidly discovering that they have been fooled by men whose aim was their own aggrandizement, not the welfare of the whole. These men cry frantically to their followers to stand fast. But why should they? Don't despond, says General Lee. But why should they not? Have the results of the war or its conduct been such as to teach them confidence?... The Richmond Examiner despairingly exclaims: "If Richmond be held but another six months the fate of the Confederacy will have been favorably decided." This was on the 27th of February, 1865; but in February, 1861, just four years before, Jefferson Davis said in Stevenson, Alabama: "Your border States will gladly come into the Southern Confederacy within sixty days, as we will be your only friends."... Do the rebel chiefs suppose that the men to whom they appeal have no sense of memory?... No wonder that half the rebel army has deserted. (*Harper's Weekly 1865a*)*

The author cleverly uses Jefferson Davis's earlier predictions about the course of the war and proves them empty. The article also uses hyperbole, thereby distorting facts—the rebel army certainly had deserters, but what evidence is offered to back up the claim that half the rebel army has deserted?

This article reverberates for us today as some Americans question whether they should trust President George W. Bush's assessment of progress in the war in Iraq. What should be the role of the press in whooping up patriotism during wartime? Is it unpatriotic or the role of good journalism to report the facts as they are? Under what circumstances does reporting the facts endanger troops on the front line? These are the kinds of questions I love to pose to students in class. In fact, I view it as my job to come up with really good questions and then to let students do the talking. If I have anything to add, it is not my own opinion but historical examples that will help clarify issues and show students what history has to teach us about events today.

To make the point about conflicting news accounts hit home, students can go online to find editorials that both support and question the president's record today (on the war or other issues). In "Using Comparative Online Media to Study the Iraq War," an article published in *Social Education* (2004), Jana Sackman Eaton suggests,

> *Compare online reports of an event related to the Iraq War from me-dia sources in a country that supported the war, a country that opposed the war, as well as a conservative and a liberal U.S. online publication. What perspectives and worldviews are reflected by the word choices, such as the adjectives and adverbs, in these reports? Which appears to be the most objective of the reports? Why? Which cite sources and appear to be the most "language neutral"? (190)*

This assignment is a useful one as students begin to write their own newspapers set in the past.

Student Newspapers: Conflicting Eyewitness Perspectives of the Same Battle

To hone in on why newspapers with different political affiliations might spin the news differently, I focus the Civil War newspaper assignment on opposing accounts of the same battle. The dateline then corresponds to the aftermath of a major battle such as Antietam (September 1862) so that each side slants its news to claim victory. First of all I want students to understand how hard it was and still is to get an accurate depiction of the facts in the immediate aftermath of a battle and to interpret the battle's effect on the course of the war without the benefit of hindsight. Although Antietam was not the decisive victory hoped for by Lee, neither was Lee's army destroyed as Lincoln had fervently wished. A good focus for conflicting newspaper accounts set during the Revolutionary War era would be the Boston Massacre or Battle of Lexington, events for which it is easy to find primary source documents from all sides claiming that the other side fired the first shot. By highlighting one battle, students begin to grasp how and by what means each side interprets events differently.

Students on both sides of conflicting Civil War newspapers on the Battle of Antietam are assigned to report on all the same topics but from different viewpoints. Several important things hung on the outcome of Antietam—whether Lee, by invading the North, could hasten the collapse of Northern resolve; whether England would recognize the Confederacy; and whether Lincoln had the victory he needed to issue the Emancipation Proclamation. Naturally, the two sides will construct different interpretations of the same events and what they portend for the future of the Civil War. While one newspaper may report a "major victory," the other may relate a "minor setback." Similar newspaper assignments could be made for battles such as Shiloh or Gettysburg.

Another option is to assign some students to write for African American or abolitionist publications. Advanced students will gain a deeper comprehension of the war by including Southern Unionist newspapers. To understand how beleaguered Lincoln was in the North, students can also publish Copperhead newspapers, whose sympathies lay with the South. However, I would not introduce too many perspectives for eighth graders and below. They easily hook into the concept of two opposing sides but most students will not be ready to see beyond that.

The list of topics to cover can be adapted to the number of students in a class such that each student must write one or more articles. Topics can address a historic event, key players in politics and warfare, and social trends. After choosing a name for itself and designing a masthead, each newspaper team can be divided into editor-in-chief, bureau chiefs, copy editors, and layout and design specialists. You can also assign department chiefs. I compose the teams such that each group has some students with excellent writing skills, some with good organizational abilities, and some with talent in the graphic arts. I ask that each major news story be accompanied by an illustration. I then let the teams assign which students will do what.

The classroom takes on a marked tone of excitement once the work begins. I spread the teams out into different corners of the room; some work in the hallways, others go off to the library, and students vie for access to the computers. I also keep a big supply of relevant books on hand and I help students locate materials relevant to their topics. Opposing sides start to jibe each other informally. Sometimes newspapers send out "spies" to see what the other side is writing about them. As long as students are working and focused, I like a room that hums with noise.

When students work in teams there is always the possibility of a dispute. Typical complaints are, "No one is listening to me," "The bossy kid is telling everyone what to do," and so-and-so "is not coming through with their share of the work." When this happens my job is to convene the team and let everyone in the group say what is on their minds. My goal is to help students listen to one another and resolve disputes. I do not see this as extraneous to my work as teacher; rather it is an important role I want to play.

Scaffolding the Newspaper Assignments for the Battle of Antietam

Students need the suggestions I provide here of *how* North and South would report on the same events through different perspectives. It saves time and it cues them into the kind of thinking I expect of them. This chart is adapted from an article I wrote for *Social Education* entitled "Students as Newspaper Reporters During the Civil War."

Battlefront
Events of the battle of Antietam, September 17, 1862
   N: Lee forced to retreat after losing one-third of his men
   S: Lee attacks the North and inflicts worst casualties yet
Robert E. Lee
   N: Traitor to his country; lost his chance on the offensive in the North
   S. Greatest military genius of the age; he will attack the North again
George B. McClellan

N: Beloved by his men; organizational genius

S: Slow-moving bungler who never seizes the advantage

The War on other fronts

N: Union blockade of South takes its toll; progress in the West

S: Brave blockade runners; counterattack in the West

Politics

Lincoln issues preliminary Emancipation Proclamation on September 22, 1862

N: A war to end slavery; negroes ready to enlist

S: Lincoln breeds insurrection among loyal slaves as a cynical war tactic

Foreign Affairs

N: On strength of Antietam and Emancipation Proclamation, England veers away from recognizing the Confederacy

S: England on the verge of recognizing our government; she will never do without our cotton

Abraham Lincoln: a biographical portrait and/or interview

N: Savior of the Union

S: Illegitimate leader and aggressor in an unnecessary war

Jefferson Davis: a biographical portrait and/or interview

N: Ineffective leader of an illegal and weak government

S: Brave leader of a new democracy fighting for its liberty

Home Front

Casualty lists and portraits of our fallen heroes (These can be modeled on real or imagined people for both the North and South.)

Home front and our women

- Work in hospitals, plantations (South) and factories (North), charities, relief societies

War industries

N: Industrial strength of our factories and railroads will help us win the war

S: Success at new industrialization; effect of blockade; inflation taking its toll

Prison camps: The horrors of prison life (both sides); eyewitness accounts from "our boys"

African Americans in the war

    N: Southern slaves desert plantations for freedom; interview with Frederick Douglass; winning the right to fight for the Union

    S: Slaves work in factories to aid our war effort; North incites our loyal slaves to flee

Entertainment and Advertisements

- Reviews of books; latest songs; fundraising events; concerts
- Serialized story of the war in the sentimental style of the day emphasizing the courage of our brave heroes and devoted women
- Illustrated advertisements for fashion, new inventions, and medical cures
- Social announcements such as marriages, births, and obituaries

Editorials

Significance of the battle

    N: England backs down from recognizing the Confederacy; Emancipation Proclamation soon to be issued; Lee's army nearly destroyed

    S: Lee inflicts heavy casualties in a daring attack on North and he will return; another show of Northern ineptitude and lack of will as our troops march on

Why we must keep fighting

    N: The Union and democracy must be saved

    S: The right to form our own government

Learning How to Write News Articles and Slant the News

This is a perfect opportunity to partner with an English teacher or to invite students on your school newspaper to talk to your class. By looking at a local or national newspaper, students can begin to identify bylines and datelines and study effective headlining. Student articles should start with a strong lead sentence that incorporates the "five W's": who, what, when, where, and why. For advice on constructing five paragraph news stories, a valuable resource is the article "Be the Press: Local Interviews, National News" by Syd Golston and Lisa Greeves, found on the NewsHour Extra website of PBS.

Before students research and write their articles I make sure they have some experience reading news stories from papers of yesteryear and studying the role of bias in reporting today. Even so I find that students initially have difficulty understanding how to slant their articles. It is hard for some students to imagine denigrating a national hero like Lincoln, even though during his lifetime he faced criticism from all sides—not only from the South, but from abolitionists as well as Copperheads. In the end, understanding how presidents like Lincoln overcame the virulent criticism facing them enhances students' appreciation of what made them so great.

I help students experiment with ways to use facts to their own advantage. For example, Tommy was assigned to write a biographical sketch of Jefferson Davis for his Northern newspaper *The State of the Union*. He told me that he did not want to include the favorable information that Davis had been a military hero in the Mexican War. After we discussed it, he came up with the following solution: "Davis distinguished himself as a colonel with the U.S. Army in our war with Mexico. Yet the traitorous leader of the Confederacy now turns his talents against the very government for whom he previously fought!" It is important for students to understand that they can slant their news stories without fabricating the facts by using a variety of propagandistic techniques. These include taking quotations out of context; overestimating enemy casualties and underestimating your own; preceding statements with leading words such as, "no more than 10,000 Southern soldiers defended the town" or "as many as 10,000 soldiers defended the town"; omitting facts; and writing headlines that arouse emotion. By using ploys such as these in their own writing, students will become more critical consumers of today's news.

A pitfall that some students fall into is doing their research and then writing it up to read like an encyclopedia entry instead of capturing the eyewitness point of view. For this reason I ask them to include quotations from interviews with foot soldiers, runaway slaves, African Americans enlisting to fight, and women in hospitals as well as from interviews with leaders and generals. As they do their research it is also important to remind students that their reading public would not have known about events subsequent to the date of publication although they might have predicted some outcomes. By forcing students to take a contemporaneous viewpoint, their writing shifts tone from the remote to the immediate.

Samples of Student Articles

When organizing the class into groups to write their newspapers I try to create balanced teams in terms of writing ability, with some very strong and some weaker writers in each group. This ensures that each paper will be edited well and that every paper will include examples of outstanding news articles. The following eyewitness account of the Battle of Gettysburg written by Ned for *The State of the Union* (July 5, 1863) falls into the average range for the eighth graders I teach. All student articles would have been typewritten in the final editions of student newspapers.

Hometown Soldier Gives Eyewitness Account of the Battle of Gettysburg

Richard Masters, the son of Rev. Everett Masters, gave The State of the Union the following exclusive interview.

I was there, I should know. I was a soldier and a fighter for our Union cause. I will tell my story as I lived it.

It was June 1863. I, Richard Masters, a soldier under the command of General George Meade, was stationed in a tiny town in Gettysburg, Pennsylvania. Confederate troops were spotted and it was not long after that our army met up with Southern cavalry led by General "Jeb" Stuart. That's where the bloodshed started. It lasted three days, from July 1, 1863 to July 3.

The first day of the battle I was stationed at the crest of a low ridge. Both armies were fighting for land, the control of hills and ridges. On the second day, I am proud to say, that we defeated the Confederate army. But there was word that Lee was planning to attack from both ends of the Union line. We could not celebrate for too long. We had to be ready for any battle planned against us. It was hard; the men of war began to get tired, but we held on fighting for what our hearts and minds believed was right.

The third day of this horrendous battle was July 3, 1863. We did not know this was the last and final day of the battle, but we thanked God when it was over. I was in the Union center, the strongest part of the Union line. This is where General Pickett attacked us in force. I felt anger and hatred towards the South because they are the ones that started this war. I will not give in until the Confederacy is defeated.

Tanisha wrote about the same battle from a Southern viewpoint for the *Charlottesville Chronicle*.

Captain James Henry, the son of a large plantation owner in Charlottesville recounted for us, "I was in Pickett's charge and it was awful. There was Union artillery and musket fire all over the place and we lost a lot of men. I suspect we lost about three fourths of all our men."

Another native son, Albert Sharron, survived the battle and told us, "I think that this setback has just told us what our objectives are, to defend the South and not to attack the North on their own ground. Furthermore, we almost defeated the North even though we were largely out numbered. This shows how superior the Southern fighting men are to the Northern fiends." Sharron recounted for this reporter how he was with Longstreet after the battle and overheard him saying, "I believe when God is on our side we cannot be defeated, and of course God is with us. I also believe that the South's greatest moment is yet to come."

You can see that in some eyes the Battle of Gettysburg can be seen as a defeat but it really is just a learning experience for the South.

Ned has done a better job than Tanisha at recounting the key events of the battle. He describes all three days rather than simply details of the third day. However, Tanisha had the harder job: to spin negative news in favor of the South. On this she did an excellent job by pointing to how well the South did even though outnumbered and to how generals would learn from this experience to better defend the South. The statement "God is on our side" captures the mentality of the day. Although neither account is as graphic as it could have been, both students breathed life into the facts by providing eyewitness accounts. I especially like the way Tanisha writes, "I suspect we lost about three quarters of our men." She is using a fact from her textbook, but one that could not be verified at the time her news article was written. Neither student provided a strong opening that gave some background information before launching into the interviews. This told me that my instructions to them could have been clearer or that I should have provided them with models for articles based on interviews.

The following excerpt from an article by Michelle for *The Southern News* published from Richmond, Virginia, is better researched. In its entirety it is almost twice as long as the previous excerpt. It reflects mastery of Lee's biography and an understanding of Lee's dignity. Michelle has a good sense for how interesting details can make her writing vivid, but a tendency to sprinkle too many commas and exclamation points throughout the piece.

> General Robert E. Lee is by far the best general in the whole Confederacy! He is the most brilliant man that even the North wanted him for commander-in-chief. When I started my interview with him, Lee came strutting in. He is a well-built man, with grey hair, and a beard. All through the interview he was most friendly.
>
> Lee was born in 1807, and his father was "Light Horse" Harry Lee. Harry Lee was the military hero of the American Revolution. He was also the Governor of Virginia, for three terms. Lee's father was not the only important Lee, two Lees were at the signing of the Declaration of Independence.
>
> Lee recounted that when he was eleven years old, his father died. Robert was left to watch over the house by himself...Robert then decided to follow in his father's footsteps, and join the army! He went to West Point, a United States Military academy, to train. Then smiling broadly Lee said, "There I graduated first in my class!" This proves that he is a great soldier...Lee informed me that he loved his estate, and his family, but he also loved army life. This love for the army usually pulled him away from his home.
>
> One day when Lee was at home with his beloved family, a lieutenant gave Lee a note saying about the attack on Harper's Ferry. Lee was ordered to command soldiers sent to take Harper's Ferry back from John Brown [in 1859].
>
> Lee said with military fire in his eyes, "John Brown was a madman. He tried to make a statement against slavery, but ended up making enemies for

his own cause"...

Then in April 1861, Lee was offered the position of General-in-chief, by Abraham Lincoln. But, he refused because he believed that the great South came first! The North wanted Lee because they, too, know that Lee is the best general, and that they would never have a general as good and talented as him.

The North still hasn't found a good a match for Lee, whose strategies, I told him, make the Northern generals run in circles! To this Lee proudly answered, "I only do my best, which the Confederacy rightly deserves!"

We are truly blessed to have such a wonderful general!

The following portrait of Jefferson Davis, written by Tommy, appeared in the *State of the Union* published in Harrisburg, Pennsylvania. It is only three paragraphs long and not as detailed as Michelle's portrait of Lee. But Tommy effectively analyzes Davis's weak points as a leader. He clearly identifies what the war is all about: slavery and the democratic process.

Jefferson Davis, the traitorous president of the rebellious Confederacy is a terrible leader, unlike Abraham Lincoln. Davis was born in 1808 in Kentucky. He was once a Senator, yet he resigned and went against the government of which he had been a part. He served in the Mexican War and was a successful colonel. Maybe that is why the South chose him for President.

The leader of the South protects the evil institution of slavery and blames the war guilt on the North. Fortunately for the Union, Davis is a poor planner and his clumsy interference in military matters is hurting the South. He kept Robert E. Lee, his best general, at a desk job for a year before giving him command of any army. He does not like to admit that he is wrong and blames his advisors for his own mistakes. For these reasons and more he is not popular with much of the South.

He refuses to trade cotton to Europe until the Confederacy is recognized as a nation. This is foolish, but helps our cause by impoverishing our opponents...Jefferson Davis does not even deserve to be leader of the Confederacy, and will never command the respect of our rightful leader, Abraham Lincoln.

During times of war, newspapers report on battles in the context of daily life on the home front. Open up the pages of a *Harper's Weekly* from the Civil War era and you can read excerpts from a novel by Charles Dickens and reports on fashion; even during the worst of times people need to be entertained. In the March 18, 1865, edition under the heading "Interesting Items," the paper reports on "A Sure Way of Procuring Pure Milk" and "Behavior at Table." Life goes on. Students learn about the important role women played in supporting the war effort when they are assigned to write about life on the home front. They can write about some of the famous women of the war, including Harriet Tubman, who worked as a scout and spy; hospital reformers Clara Barton and Dorothea Dix; camp followers; and spies like Rose O'Neal Greenhow and Belle Boyd. There were also women who fought disguised as men.

Some of America's most famous writers, such as Walt Whitman and Louisa May Alcott, worked and wrote about their experiences in hospitals during the Civil War. Their accounts make good models for student writing. Below is Whitman's dispatch to the New York Times on December 11, 1864.

> *They are breaking up the camp hospitals in Meade's Army, preparing for a move. As I write this, in March, there are all the signs. Yesterday and last night the sick were arriving here in long trains, all day and night. I was among the newcomers most of the night. One train of a thousand came into the depot and others followed. The ambulances were going all night, distributing them to the various hospitals here…When they come in, some literally in a dying condition, you may well imagine it is a lamentable sight…A wanderer like me about Washington pauses on some high land which commands the sweep of the city…Counting the whole, with the convalescent camps (whose inmates are often worse off than the sick in the hospitals)…they have numbered in this quarter and just down the Potomac as high as fifty thousand invalid, disabled, or sick and dying men. ([1864] 1960, 70–71)*

For a Northern newspaper, my student Louis incorporated what he had learned from reading Walt Whitman into his own account of the home front.

> Let no one underestimate the suffering that we Northerners have experi-
> enced during this terrible war. It is impossible to avoid the war in the North,
> even though everyone wishes they could, because they are haunted by the
> absence of their loved ones until they return. When a member of a family
> goes away to war there is no telling when they will be back again and if they
> are lucky enough to return who knows what shape they will be in...Soldiers
> from the battlefield have told this reporter that wounded men are lucky to
> be found on the day they are injured. When they are found they are either
> taken to a hospital or a church or somebody's home...As I have traveled the
> battlefronts, I have been amazed to see that these types of shelters and
> hospitals are always full. At one point these shelters were filled with 50,000
> people. Walt Whitman remarked to me, "This number is more numerous in
> itself than the Washington of ten or fifteen years ago."

While most of the writing here is not particularly vivid, the way that
Louis quotes Walt Whitman, thereby putting the number of 50,000
wounded in the total context of Washington's population, makes it truly a
chilling figure.

Analyzing Advertisements as Primary Source Documents

If I had my druthers, all the graphics for student newspapers would
be hand drawn. Students learn a tremendous amount from sketching,
because it forces them to spend time looking at the models from which
they are copying, whether they be the drawings of Winslow Homer
reprinted in *Harper's Weekly* or the advertisements for patent medicines,
sewing machines, pianos, or the latest clothing fashions. But with access
to the Internet from which students can cut and paste images into their
newspapers, the likelihood is that newspaper graphics will end up being a
"cut and paste" job.

My students learn that I am something of a stickler when it comes to
history. They do not mind this because they know it comes from my delight
in historical detail—and I want that to become infectious. So even if I let

students cut and paste advertisements from the Web, I use the opportunity to teach them a thing or two about the technological advances that enabled newspapers to print graphics. These advances led to the inclusion of more advertisements and larger format pages. Matthew Brady photographed the Civil War, but the technology did not yet exist for reprinting his work en masse in the press. Lithographed sketches were the order of the day during the Civil War, so if students download images I want them to find lithographs, not photographs! Newspaper assignments set after the 1890s can authentically include photographs. It is imperative that students turn in a bibliography that lists the online sources of their graphic material.

How else can I ensure that students learn something from the images they find and choose to include? One way is to teach students how to analyze graphics as primary source documents before they incorporate them as part of their newspapers. As documents go, advertisements are among the most fun to analyze. A great way to start is to ask students to read and complete the exercises in "Making Sense of Advertisements," written by historian Daniel Pope and available online at the History Matters website (see Appendix E). In the carefully sequenced activities Pope designed, students learn to identify the purpose of an ad and the methods it uses to grab our attention. Pope cautions us not to view an advertisement apart from its context, and to look for what is unstated as well as missing. He writes:

> *In examining ads as historical documents, we also should look at what the ad seems to take for granted. Inferring social conditions from advertisements is not straightforward. Ads are highly selective in their depiction of the world. Notably, historical and contemporary studies abound showing that advertising's depiction of American society has been highly skewed in its portrayal of race, class, and gender.*
>
> *Until a generation ago, African Americans and other people of color were virtually invisible in mainstream advertising, except when they were portrayed as servants or as exemplifying racially stereotyped behavior…Images of women in advertising have hardly been uniform, but several themes recur: the housewife ecstatic over a new cleaning product; the anxious woman fearing the loss of youthful attractiveness; the subservient spouse dependent on her assertive husband; the object*

of men's sexual gaze and desire…Advertising also gives false testimony about the actual class structure of American society. Advertising images consistently show scenes of prosperity, material comfort, even luxury well beyond the conditions of life of most Americans. The advertising industry prefers to picture the world that consumers aspire to, not the one they actually inhabit. (Pope)

Advertisements tell us what we have in common with our ancestors—a fear of premature hair loss, a desire for perfectly fitting shirts—but also how we differ from them. The myriad advertisements for farm products in *Harper's Weekly*, published in New York, remind us of how agrarian the nation still was. We no longer need to rely on quack remedies. The numerous and ever-increasing number of advertisements for runaway slaves in Civil War newspapers from the South are a potent indicator of what the war was all about. They demonstrate that the high-minded rhetoric of freedom for the South meant freedom for the "right" to own slaves. They also testify to the courage of enslaved Africans in pursuit of attaining their freedom. Many of the runaways eventually fought for the Union.

I like to model with my students how to analyze historical advertisements, but they have more fun doing it first with advertisements from current publications. Then we move on to ads from the time period under consideration (see Figure 5.2). In both cases I require that they fill out the Advertisement Analysis Worksheet I designed (see Figure 5.3 and Appendix I) to accompany the ads they cut and paste from the Internet or photocopy from books. This way I know they have learned something significant. I also give them a Cartoon Analysis Worksheet, which is discussed in Chapter 6.

Producing the Student Newspapers in Class

Student-produced newspapers should go through the stages of any publication, including the writing of drafts, rewrites, and copy editing. Although this is time consuming, the newspaper assignment has many things working in its favor to reduce the work of the teacher. First is the fact that students are already working together on teams that model how real newspapers are written, and each person's work should be read,

Fig 5.2 From advertisements students can learn how similar and different life in the past was to life today.

commented on, and proofread by several other team members. In fact, frequent rereading of the articles will help students master the historical content as well as improve their writing skills. Set-ups can include a first reading by the editor-in-chief, whose task it is to comment on and improve the content of each article, while copy editors can proofread for grammar, spelling, and punctuation.

This is a perfect assignment for the social studies, English, or computer teacher to introduce the use of "track changes" to students. Track changes is a feature in Microsoft Word and is used widely in the business world. Students submit their early drafts to one another on the computer, and the student who edits the articles makes or suggests changes that are highlighted in red and sends the article back to its author. The author accepts, rejects, and amends the piece of writing accordingly. The last and final version can be emailed to the teacher for final touch-ups. The students and teacher alike can use the rubrics provided at the end of this chapter.

Newspapers can be printed and distributed in numerous ways. A computer program like Adobe PageMaker can be used for formatting and integrating all the news articles and visuals. Alternatively, students can cut and paste their columns onto master sheets. I actually prefer this method for Civil War newspapers because we can lay them out and print them up on eleven-by-seventeen-inch sheets of paper that are roughly the same size as *Harper's Weekly*. Ideally, copies of all the newspapers should be photocopied for every student to read. If this is not possible, students should receive a copy of the paper they worked on and one other paper representing an opposing viewpoint. Another option is to post the newspapers on the school website so that they can all be read online.

		Advertisement Analysis Worksheet
A.		In what publication did this advertisement appear? What is the date of publication?
B.		Who created the advertisement?
C.		What is the purpose of the advertisement?
D.		Who is the intended audience for the advertisement?
E.		If a product is being sold, what strategies does the ad use to convince the target audience that they should want this product?
F.		How common or unique was this product for its era?
G.		What does the advertisement tell us about material life in America at this time?
H.		What does the advertisement tell us about social relationships in America at this time?

Fig 5.3 Advertisement Analysis Worksheet

Conflicting Newspapers Set in Other Time Periods

There are many ways to incorporate and adapt conflicting newspaper accounts into various units of study. One way is to have students write conflicting interpretations of the same events as articles within the same newspaper. This is what I assigned for a unit on the 1920s. My focus was the Scopes Trial and the rapid social and material changes of the time period. In English class, students read the fictionalized version of the Scope's trial, *Inherit the Wind*, and studied journalism of the period, which by now aimed

Fig 5.4 This page from a student-made 1925 newspaper on the Scopes Trial shows that students have captured the zeitgeist of the period in their original artwork.

Fig 5.5 From prohibition to Ku Klux Klan activity to controversy over Darwinism, this page demonstrates that students understood life in the 1920s.

at greater objectivity than it did during the nineteenth century. They also used the news articles of H. L. Mencken as primary source documents on which to model their writing. In this student newspaper, the "battlefront" was the Scopes trial itself. I assigned topics designed to elucidate the rapid technological and social changes in the 1920s and the backlash they elicited from many Americans—including a rejection of modern science. Students wrote articles about women winning the vote, a visit to Harlem, the rise of the Ku Klux Klan, the effect of the automobile, Prohibition, the high tide of immigration and legislation to end it, and the financial boom.

Yet another model for conflicting newspapers is to create assignments that explore multiple perspectives within a minority of the public. For example, competing newspapers set in 1912 can voice opposing strategies for how women can most effectively gain the right to vote. This issue divided suffragist organizations at different times in history, but especially so during Woodrow Wilson's presidency. Students can write newspapers that advocate for one organization over another, demonstrating that a movement that shared one goal was divided over the best strategies for attaining it.

Wilson's presidency also saw the rise of powerful newspapers written for and by African Americans. These included *The Crisis* edited by W. E. B. DuBois, which was written to combat Booker T. Washington's accommodationist stance to racial oppression, and Robert Abbott's *Chicago Defender*, which focused its wrath on racial injustices in the South, especially Jim Crow laws and lynching. It encouraged Southern blacks to move North. The *Boston Guardian* was edited by William Monroe Trotter, who, unlike DuBois, believed the effort to achieve racial equality should come without the help of white patrons. While covering some of the same ground, each of these influential newspapers took a different tack. Taken together, a set of student newspapers advocating racial equality and women's rights would illuminate a great deal about the Progressive Era and Wilson's presidency. For information on implementing these ideas, see the PBS website for the American Experience program, *Woodrow Wilson*.

Newspaper assignments can also be useful when studying immigration by asking students to replicate the presses of ethnic groups in America. Different teams can be assigned to create newspapers that advocate for specific ethnic groups. The headline news of the day could be the passage of the Immigration Act of 1924, which closed America's doors to immigrants of many ethnicities. Each ethnic newspaper could then highlight the impact the act would have on its readership. The Triangle Shirtwaist factory fire of 1911 would make another good headline for this assignment. Newspapers published for and by different ethnic groups are easy to come by in large cities today; many are published online. Historical publications such as *The Jewish Daily Forward* or *The Irish Echo* can be used as primary source models for such student-created publications.

Sharing What Students Learn

Once newspapers are distributed they should become interactive springboards to student debate and discussion. Like other eyewitness strategies, this one places political and military history in the context of social history. Because all students are contributing to the final product, more information is being generated. Students should thus master more than what they write about as individuals. To ensure that students do so, it is important that the newspapers are read and used. Implementing one of the suggested activities in this section will ensure that this happens.

Holding Debates and Symposiums

Because key historical figures are presented in the news from conflicting viewpoints, it is easy to move on to formalized debate about them. For the Civil War newspaper a good example would be to debate the proposition, "Resolved: That Robert E. Lee is a great American hero." You can stipulate that all information used in the debate must draw on student articles. To challenge students even more, you can turn the tables and ask students to switch sides and support the viewpoint they did not already write about.

For a newspaper assignment that explores different strategies for attaining the same goal—suffrage for women or civil rights for African Americans, for example—the class can convene a symposium of all "staff writers" from their papers. The symposium participants must resolve their differences and agree to use one approach or develop a compromise based on several approaches in order to attain their goal. For a model of how to hold a conflict resolution session you can adapt the Choices Program model developed at Brown University (see Appendix E, "Choices for the 21st Century"). To prepare for the symposium, students need to carefully read the newspapers of all the organizations represented at the table.

Writing Letters to the Editors

Another interactive route to engage students in what their classmates have written is to ask each student to write a letter to the editor of an opposing viewpoint newspaper. Letters can question the accuracy of a news article and/or challenge the opinion of its authors. Letters to the editor are written from the eyewitness perspective; in other words, students do not represent themselves living today but write as eyewitnesses to the events of yesteryear. After the letters are distributed to the appropriate teams, newspaper staffs convene to read the letters and write responses to them. Knowing that their news articles can be challenged in this fashion keeps students on their toes as they write them. The newspapers, letters to the editors, and responses can be read aloud in dramatic form or be displayed on a bulletin board.

Holding a Press Award Ceremony

A less interactive but still engaging method to assure that students read and learn from their classmates' newspapers is to hold a press award ceremony. A number of prizes can be awarded in numerous categories, such as best written article, best graphic award, and most comprehensive news coverage. Teams from the North, for example, can be the judges of newspapers written in the South. Some students work hardest when they know such a ceremony will be held at the end.

Assessment

The eyewitness newspaper assignment requires team effort and collaboration on the part of students, unlike the previous eyewitness strategies in which students worked alone or with partners. In the previous strategies, they created personas through whose eyes they saw events. They developed a personal narrative in response to factual events. Creating a story line helps students imagine the past because it harnesses their adolescent egocentric outlook.

In the eyewitness newspaper assignment, the emphasis shifts and becomes more sophisticated. Students write as journalists for a public audience. However, they still hold assigned political viewpoints that they represent in their articles. They must also cooperate on teams, fulfilling a variety of roles in order to produce a joint product. The rubrics below therefore include cooperative learning categories. Teachers can grade students on their individual contributions, the team effort (the newspaper they produce), or both.

Newspaper Rubrics

Rubric for Individual Student

Topic	Criteria	Mark from 1–5
Writing, Technical	Do you use correct spelling, grammar, punctuation, and syntax?	
Journalistic Writing	Do your news articles cover the 5 W's: who, what, when, where, and why? Do you write from an eyewitness perspective? Do you capture the journalistic style of the period?	
News Articles	Do you convey accurate and relevant historical information? Do you provide vivid factual details? Do you effectively represent your viewpoint?	
Advertisements	Are your advertisement(s) appropriate for the time period and do they reflect something about it? Have you successfully completed an Advertisement Analysis Worksheet for each ad you downloaded? If you drew ads, were they artful and done with care?	
Collaborative Team Effort	Did you take an active role in team planning? Were you responsible about fulfilling team roles? Did you comment on and edit other students' work effectively?	
Overall Comment	Did you contribute regularly to class discussion? Did you effectively represent your side's viewpoint of the conflict?	

Rubric for Newspaper Team

Topic	Criteria	Mark from 1–5
Writing, Technical	Did the articles in your newspaper use correct spelling, grammar, punctuation, and syntax?	
Journalistic Writing	Did your news articles cover the 5 W's: who, what, when, where, and why? Were they written from an eyewitness perspective? Did they capture the journalistic style of the period?	
News Articles	Does your newspaper convey accurate and relevant historical information? Does it provide vivid factual details? Does it effectively represent your team's viewpoint?	
Advertisements	Are your advertisement(s) appropriate for the time period and do they reflect something about it? Have you successfully completed an Advertisement Analysis Worksheet for each ad your team downloaded? If you drew ads, were they artful and done with care?	
Collaborative Team Effort	Did your team work effectively together? Did group members take initiative and follow through on group decisions? Did you effectively resolve problems as a team?	
Layout and Final Product	Is your newspaper visually pleasing and effective? Is the layout clean, consistent, and easy to follow?	
Overall Comment		

Chapter Six

Election Speeches: Advocating for Your Candidate

Most of the problems a president has to face have their roots in the past.

President Harry Truman, 1956

Every four years presidential elections are the subject of intense scrutiny and debate, not only in the media, but also in classrooms across the country. All our students have lived through at least one election memorable for its excitement, drama, and the increasing frenzy as election day nears. Students understand that who becomes president has a direct impact on their lives, and after the disputed election of 2000, we know that even a handful of votes can be of enormous consequence in deciding the nation's future.

Learning about elections in American history can be equally exciting if only teachers can learn to transfer this ready-made and exciting scenario to a study of elections past. My own experience has taught me that restaging an election can electrify students, injecting partisanship and passion into their study of the candidates and the issues they represented. Meanwhile, students gain a better understanding of many fundamental themes that have been important throughout American history.

The idea behind an election debate is quite simple: divide the class into adherents for the historical candidates and let them run campaigns, win votes, and hold debates as supporters living during the time period. Student-created campaign banners, paraphernalia, songs, and especially speeches all play a role. Documents from the time period, including both written ones and visual artifacts, provide models that illuminate the issues and campaign strategies.

As might be expected, some students go along with this game plan reluctantly since they can flip open their textbooks to see who really won. This can be true especially of competitive students. Philip was a boy in my class who always wanted to be on the winning side, so when I put him on the team of a candidate who never became president he was very disappointed. He thought he was on the losing side from the start, and he had trouble staying motivated. But when I told him that who wins or loses *our election* depends only on how well he and his teammates make their case, he became infected with campaign fever right away. Rewriting history can be both fun and informative.

There are many elections that can be successfully restaged in the classroom. The rivalry between John Adams and Thomas Jefferson in the campaign of 1800 makes a good start, especially because it lays the basis for understanding the origins of party politics in the new republic. It also helps students understand the need for passage of the Twelfth Amendment, which changed the election procedure for president and vice president. (Up until then the runner-up for president became vice president.) Students can learn a great deal by studying history's great losers, like Henry Clay and William Jennings Bryan, who each ran for president three times and failed. The Lincoln-Douglas debates (although they occurred during a race for the Senate) are important for understanding how great speeches are constructed. The Stolen Election of 1876, when Rutherford B. Hayes ran against Samuel Tilden, makes it clear just how much went wrong at the end of Reconstruction. It is also possible to stage a variety of campaigns in which more than two parties ran strong candidates. This happened in the three-way race of 1912 among Woodrow Wilson, Teddy Roosevelt, and Howard Taft. The election of 1928 between Herbert Hoover and Alfred E. Smith (the first Catholic to run for president) illuminates important aspects of the social history of the twenties. The first televised debates, between Richard Nixon and John F. Kennedy in 1960, set the precedent for today's presidential debates.

Studying campaigns from different time periods also sheds light on the history of suffrage in the United States and the ways in which technology has transformed the campaigning process itself. Because presidential candidates of the major parties have been exclusively white Christian males, my class discusses the role and power (or lack thereof) of minorities and women as voters and candidates.

The art of oratory takes center stage in this eyewitness strategy, literally and figuratively. Letters and diaries are private matters. Newspaper articles are written for the public to read; speeches are written for the public to *hear*. More than any other genre discussed in this book, speeches are carefully constructed arguments aimed at convincing an audience to make a choice. The primary sources I use as models for this strategy are speeches written by the candidates themselves or their contemporaries on important issues of the day. Nowadays the Web provides a wealth of ways to actually listen to some of the great oratory of the twentieth century.

Organizing an Election Debate

One thing I have learned over time: there are multiple ways to organize an election debate. My choice of debate model depends on a number of factors. First, How many students do I want to participate in the debate itself? What will be the role of the remaining students in the class? What debate format do I want to follow? Who will judge which side election, and on what basis will this decision be made?

In general I like students to work in teams of four to Teamwork builds a sense of responsibility that no amount parents or teachers can match. I remember one student who was charming and personable, but too satisfied with mediocre work. I knew he could do better, but nothing I did to motivate him seemed to work. When he was part of a debate team to get Andrew Jackson reelected in 1832, he likewise put minimal effort into the early drafts of his speech— until his teammates got after him. They wanted to win the election, and they knew that if Gary did not come through with his best effort their chances were minimized. It was peer pressure that finally got him going in

138 | 139

earnest. I have seen other students grow so passionate about their candidate that they surprised themselves by how hard they worked on his behalf!

In some models of presidential debates, students reenact the presidential candidates themselves, with the rest of the group playing supporting roles. I prefer not to use this model because I don't like to elevate some students to "starring roles." (Even through the 1830s it was deemed unseemly for the candidates themselves to campaign anyway!) In some years I make exceptions when I know I have two students who will make stellar candidates without wanting to steal the show. But in general I do not follow this model.

If the candidates don't make appearances in most of my election debates, how do they work? In effect, students become local supporters of their candidate, out to convince their friends and neighbors to get out and vote. Each member of the team is assigned to take on one aspect of his or her candidate's platform. A student on the opposing team will take on that same issue from the perspective of the opposing candidate's platform. In other words, there may be five one-on-one debates, each one about a specific aspect of the candidates' platforms. Each minidebate is a timed exchange of constructive speeches, in which students set forth their arguments alternating with rebuttal speeches in which they refute their opponents' arguments. But together each team must strategize, present a variety of campaign literature and paraphernalia (cartoons, buttons, and posters), build a unified line of argument, and support one another in a variety of ways. In the end, the team that has convinced the audience that its candidate deserves to be president is the winning team. At the end of this chapter I suggest some ways to score such a debate.

I have used or adapted other models of debate as well. Sometimes I replace rebuttal speeches with a question and answer format. This works especially well in three-way races. Speakers for candidates A, B, and C present their constructive speeches on a particular topic. Then a member of team A and B each pose a question to speaker C that C answers. Next, speakers B and C pose questions to speaker A and so forth. Alternatively, questions can be asked by a moderator or by students role-playing members of the press or the "voters" themselves. All of these models have precedents in recent times, and students may have watched a number of "town meeting" style debates on television. I like these formats because they emphasize the role of citizens in probing the issues.

If only some of the students participate in the actual debate, what do the others do? They can become the voters or judges, but this does not necessarily take much work or give them experience debating. So I might supplement their roles as voters by asking them to create classroom materials for our bulletin boards, such as time lines of the candidates' lives or maps of states included in the Union at the time of the election. Or I might not give the rest of the class any extra work until later in the year, when a different group of students gets to stage an election debate from a later period of U.S. history. In general, I want every student to learn how to write a speech and debate an issue by year's end.

Because a debate is a competitive activity, I create balanced teams. Each group needs some dynamic speakers and hard workers, as well as students who foster cooperation. Gifted artists also get to help their team win because the campaign paraphernalia they create wins points, too. Given all these considerations, I cannot assign each student to support their first-choice candidate. I remind students of a few things that help assuage any disappointment. Learning to make a good argument is an important skill to master. Lawyers are trained to make the best case they can for their clients, regardless of how they feel about them personally. Students usually understand this to some extent from watching television programs. I also remind the class that in competitive high school debate, teams are not told which side of an argument they must support until just before the debate starts. This means they must arrive ready to support both sides of the argument. And because they have already thought through arguments on both sides of the issues, they are much better prepared to make their rebuttals.

Speeches as Primary Documents

I most like to set an election debate during what is known as "the golden age of American oratory," between the campaigns of 1828 and 1860. Students are always struck by photographs of its three oratorical giants—the fanatical and fiery looking John C. Calhoun, the haunting, dark-eyed Daniel Webster, the mild-mannered face of Henry Clay, "the Great Compromiser." According to Lillian O'Connor (1954), "Small wonder also that at that moment in history woman recollected that she, too, had had the gift of speech bestowed upon her by her Maker and that she, too, might use it in behalf of those who had the least opportunity to enjoy life, liberty, and the pursuit of happiness: the Southern slave" (124). This is the time period when women like Sarah and Angelina Grimké and Sojourner Truth came out of the parlor to speak in public (quite shockingly at the time) to "promiscuous audiences" of both men and women. If women and African Americans were disenfranchised, at least they could use their First Amendment rights to speak, publish, and petition. Frederick Douglass ends his *Narrative of the Life of Frederick Douglass* ([1845] 2003) by recounting the first time he pled the cause of freedom to an audience of white abolitionists. "I spoke but a few moments, when I felt a degree of freedom, and said what I desired with considerable ease. From that time until now, I have been engaged in pleading the case of my brethren" (119). Asking students to imagine what it would be like to meet or hear one of these awe-inspiring orators is a good exercise in itself.

Analyzing Speeches

Before asking students to write speeches on specific issues in support of their candidate, I want them to analyze a selection of great speeches to see how they are constructed. Unlike other primary source documents presented in this book that were written only to be read, speeches were written to be delivered aloud to an audience. When studying examples in class I read the speech aloud, mustering as much flourish as possible, or I ask some students to prepare a historical speech as a dramatic monologue. They can read it, or better yet memorize it, and deliver it in persona with at least a few suggestive props or costume items such as a cane, stiff white collar, bonnet, or top hat. This is a good opportunity to invite a drama teacher to work collaboratively with you. Those long Victorian sentences can be very difficult for students to understand on the page; hearing them out loud makes them immediately more accessible. By staging the speech, words and even setting come to life.

I remind students that when analyzing a speech, the document cannot be thought of in isolation from its intended audience. What was the speaker's goal vis-a-vis his or her listeners? By looking at a selection of speeches from the time period, students can become more adept at analyzing them and writing their own.

The art of rhetoric was held in high esteem in nineteenth-century America. According to Gregory Clark and S. Michael Halloran (1993), "The rhetoric taught in American colleges at the beginning of the nineteenth century was strongly neoclassical, which is to say that it was a rhetoric of general citizenship closely tied to the public discourse practiced in pulpit, bar, and senate of the larger society" (6). Rhetoric is argument whose goal is to persuade. According to Aristotle, there are three modes of proof: (1) The speaker must win our confidence by his intelligence and moral character; (2) he must win our emotional support; and (3) he must persuade through logical argument. I like students to get a taste of what Aristotle meant by these categories before they begin.

In terms of winning the confidence of their listeners, women who took the podium broke the rules of their patriarchal society and were thus immediately suspected of bad moral character. In the nineteenth century the intelligence of both women and African Americans was questioned. They had a special burden to convince the audience of their worth as witnesses.

This opening of a speech delivered by abolitionist and feminist Angelina Grimké at Pennsylvania Hall in 1838 demonstrates how she handled this situation. (The speech can be found on the website for *Africans in America* at PBS. See Appendix F.)

Men, brethren and fathers—mothers, daughters and sisters, what came ye out for to see? A reed shaken with the wind? Is it curiosity merely, or a deep sympathy with the perishing slave, that has brought this large audience together? [A yell from the mob without the building.] Those voices without ought to awaken and call out our warmest sympathies. Deluded beings! "they know not what they do." They know not that they are undermining their own rights and their own happiness, temporal and eternal. Do you ask, "what has the North to do with slavery?" Hear it—hear it. Those voices without tell us that the spirit of slavery is here, and has been roused to wrath by our abolition speeches and conventions: for surely liberty would not foam and tear herself with rage, because her friends are multiplied daily, and meetings are held in quick succession to set forth her virtues and extend her peaceful kingdom. This opposition shows that slavery has done its deadliest work in the hearts of our citizens. Do you ask, then, "what has the North to do?" I answer, cast out first the spirit of slavery from your own hearts, and then lend your aid to convert the South.

As a Southerner I feel that it is my duty to stand up here to-night and bear testimony against slavery. I have seen it—I have seen it. I know it has horrors that can never be described. I was brought up under its wing: I witnessed for many years its demoralizing influences, and its destructiveness to human happiness. It is admitted by some that the slave is not happy under the worst *forms of slavery. But I have never* seen a happy slave.

Reading this speech we can easily imagine the audience in the hall as well as the hecklers outside. You can even ask some students to get out of their seats and *be* those hecklers as the speech is read to the class. What would the hecklers be saying? Grimké addresses her audience directly as if they were seated in pews segregated by sex. Instead of, "Men and women, brothers and sisters," she says, "Men, brethren, and fathers," first. As if to acknowledge that she has broken gender rules she says, "What came ye out for to see? A reed shaken with the wind?" which is a biblical quote from the book of Matthew. By alluding to biblical passages throughout her speech, Grimké establishes her credentials as a good Christian woman, someone whose words deserve to be heeded even if she has broken with convention by speaking to "promiscuous" audiences.

Grimké strengthens our willingness to credit her knowledge of slavery by saying, "As a Southerner I feel that it is my duty to stand up here to-night and bear testimony against slavery. I have seen it—I have seen it." Thus, despite her deficits as a female speaker, she has fulfilled what Aristotle called ethical proof: the trustworthiness of the speaker. Grimké's charge to her audience is clear at the outset: to "Cast out first the spirit of slavery from your own hearts, and then lend your aid to convert the South." In the first instance listeners must come to terms with their own prejudices, in the second take action. Grimké cleverly uses the rabble-rousers outside the hall as proof that the evils of slavery have infected not only the South, but the North as well.

A speech delivered by Frederick Douglass on Independence Day in

July, 1852, in Rochester, New York, is a good example of how a great speaker wins our emotional support. (The complete text of this speech can be found on the website of the Douglass Archives of American Public Address. See Appendix F.) Douglass starts by flattering the intelligence of the audience relative to the speaker's (a sure way to win over adversaries) and goes on to rouse patriotic fervor by reviewing the events leading up to the American Revolution:

> *Oppression makes a wise man mad. Your fathers were wise men, and if they did not go mad, they became restive under this treatment [by Great Britain]. They felt themselves the victims of grievous wrongs, wholly incurable in their colonial capacity. With brave men there is always a remedy for oppression. Just here, the idea of a total separation of the colonies from the crown was born! It was a startling idea, much more so, than we, at this distance of time, regard it. The timid and the prudent (as has been intimated) of that day, were, of course, shocked and alarmed by it. (Douglass 1852)*

Douglass's intention is make the audience feel proud of what their forebears accomplished, and I can imagine a few listeners feeling rather puffed up by Douglass's words of praise for their ancestors. But then Douglass takes an unexpected turn, by pointing out what the Independence Day celebration means to the slave:

> *What, to the American slave, is your 4th of July? I answer: a day that reveals to him, more than all other days in the year, the gross injustice and cruelty to which he is the constant victim. To him, your celebration is a sham; your boasted liberty, an unholy license; your national greatness, swelling vanity; your sounds of rejoicing are empty and heartless; your denunciations of tyrants, brass fronted impudence; your shouts of liberty and equality, hollow mockery; your prayers and hymns, your sermons and thanksgivings, with all your religious parade, and solemnity, are, to him, mere bombast, fraud, deception, impiety, and hypocrisy—a thin veil to cover up crimes which would disgrace a nation of savages. There is not a nation on the earth guilty of practices,*

more shocking and bloody, than are the people of these United States, at this very hour. (Douglass 1852)

Although at first Douglass played on feelings of pride among his audience members, he now twists that very feeling and turns it into a source of shame. To the slave, "Your celebration is a sham; your boasted liberty, an unholy license." By touching our emotions (Aristotle's "pathetic proof") Douglass has exposed the hypocrisy of a patriotic holiday. Douglass is a master of parallel constructions; behind every positive epithet used to describe the United States, he uncovers its opposite, until he ends with a groundswell of condemnatory adjectives.

Just a small extract from a lengthy speech by Daniel Webster, delivered to the Senate on March 7, 1850, can illustrate for students the final and most important aspect of persuasive speech: Aristotle's logical proof. In this famous address (reprinted in full on the website of Dartmouth College; see Appendix F), Webster argued in support of the Compromise of 1850, which among other things strengthened the fugitive slave clause of the U.S. Constitution. He feared that without compromise the dissolution of the Union would be imminent. Here he condemns the abolitionists:

Then, Sir, there are the Abolition societies, of which I am unwilling to speak, but in regard to which I have very clear notions and opinions. I do not think them useful. I think their operations for the last twenty years have produced nothing good or valuable. At the same time, I believe thousands of their members to be honest and good men, perfectly well-meaning men. They have excited feelings; they think they must do something for the cause of liberty; and, in their sphere of action, they do not see what else they can do than to contribute to an Abolition press, or an Abolition society, or to pay an Abolition lecturer. I do not mean to impute gross motives even to the leaders of these societies, but I am not blind to the consequences of their proceedings. I cannot but see what mischiefs their interference with the South has produced. And is it not plain to every man? Let any gentleman who entertains doubts on this point recur to the debates in the Virginia House of Delegates in 1832, and he will see with what freedom a proposition made by Mr.[Thomas]

Jefferson Randolph for the gradual abolition of slavery was discussed in that body. Every one spoke of slavery as he thought; very ignominious and disparaging names and epithets were applied to it. The debates in the House of Delegates on that occasion, I believe, were all published. They were read by every colored man who could read, and to those who could not read, those debates were read by others. At that time Virginia was not unwilling or unafraid to discuss this question, and to let that part of her population know as much of discussion as they could learn. That was in 1832. As has been said by the honorable member from South Carolina [Calhoun], these Abolition societies commenced their course of action in 1835. It is said, I do not know how true it may be, that they sent incendiary publications into the slave States; at any rate, they attempted to arouse, and did arouse, a very strong feeling; in other words, they created great agitation in the North against Southern slavery.

Well, what was the result? The bonds of the slave were bound more firmly than before, their rivets were more strongly fastened. Public opinion, which in Virginia had begun to be exhibited against slavery, and was opening out for the discussion of the question, drew back and shut itself up in its castle. I wish to know whether any body in Virginia can now talk openly as Mr. Randoph, Governor [James] McDowell, and others talked in 1832 and sent their remarks to the press? We all know the fact, and we all know the cause; and every thing that these agitating people have done has been, not to enlarge, but to restrain, not to set free, but to bind faster the slave population of the South. (Webster 1850)

Because abolitionists are unequivocally lauded in today's textbooks, students are usually surprised to learn that in their day they were hated not only by Southerners, but by most Northerners as well. Even the American history textbook I read as an eighth grader criticized abolitionists as rabble-rousers who polarized the country—the same argument that was being used in the early 1960s to condemn leaders such as Martin Luther King Jr. Despite their surprise at Webster's criticism of the abolitionists, students concede that they must take his argument seriously and dissect it point for point. I like them to notice how Webster does not vilify the cause of the abolitionists, but shows their means to be counterproductive: "I cannot but see what mischiefs their interference with the South has produced." Using the chart below, I ask the class to list each argument Webster makes and the facts he offers in support of it. He claims, "The bonds of the slave were bound more firmly than before," but does not offer concrete evidence to back it up. He is better at supporting his contention that there was more open discussion about ending slavery before the abolitionists "excited feelings."

Webster's Contentions	Webster's Supporting Evidence	Student Rebuttal: Contentions	Student Rebuttal: Supporting Evidence (to find)

Now I ask students to pretend they are debating Webster. How will they refute his arguments? What will their contentions be? Can they show that the abolitionists were creating better conditions for the slave in the short term? Did that matter if the abolitionists were bringing the nation closer to abolishing slavery altogether? What reasons and facts will students use to support their ideas? If they do not have the information they need, where will they get it? A small exercise like this can put students in a frame of mind to debate.

For an extensive exposure to the art of debate, nothing can compare to the Lincoln-Douglas debates of 1858. I like to use the debates as they appear in play form in Act III, Scene 9, of Robert E. Sherwood's *Abe Lincoln in Illinois*. In this version we see the speaker's platform, Lincoln taking notes while Douglas speaks, and a moderator introducing the speakers, thus bringing the words to life in its setting. This intellectual dueling match is wonderful to teach because students can follow how both men put forth arguments and defended them, point for point. Applying the model I suggest above, I give students one of Douglas's arguments and ask them to devise a good rebuttal. For example, Douglas claims that the industrial workers in the North often have worse living conditions than slaves in the South. We can then compare their responses to the one that Lincoln gave (in the play):

> *I can assure Judge Douglas that I have been there, and I have seen those cheerless brick prisons called factories and the workers trudging silently home through the darkness. In those factories cotton that was picked by black slaves is woven into cloth by white people who are separated from slavery by no more than fifty cents a day. As an American, I cannot be proud that such conditions exist. But also as an American, I can ask, would any of those striking workers in the North elect to change places with the slaves in the South? Will they not rather say, "The remedy is in our hands!" And still as an American I can say, thank God we live under a system by which men have the right to strike! (Sherwood 1937, 62)*

By looking at a variety of primary source speeches delivered during the antebellum era, students can learn what they need to accomplish in their own speeches: to comport themselves in a manner that wins trust and demonstrates expertise, to strive to gain the emotional support of the audience, and finally to persuade the audience through reasoned argument to vote for their candidate.

Choosing an Election and Defining the Issues

No matter what election we reenact, I try to focus on issues that will draw on students' prior knowledge of U.S. history and its founding documents. For any presidential election debate it is important for students to define the characteristics of a good leader. I ask every student in the class to write down one characteristic he or she thinks is important. We then list all of the characteristics on the board and try to rank them through

group consensus—a great class, right there. Is military experience always important? What about education? How important is travel abroad? As always, I never give my own opinion because that only discourages students from formulating their own ideas and sharing them. But I might add a historical fact to the debate, such as, "Woodrow Wilson saw us through World War I without ever having served in the armed forces himself" or, "Dwight D. Eisenhower became president after being a general." Following this discussion I give students one-page biographies of the candidates we are going to campaign for and ask them to list the pros and cons of each candidate in light of the previous discussion about good leadership. Already a lot of excitement has been generated for staging our own election campaign.

Because the oath of office requires the president to "protect, preserve, and defend the Constitution of the United States," students need to understand the powers of the presidency as defined by the U.S. Constitution. They are easily confused by the inflated and often repeated campaign promises many candidates make today, which lead them to believe the president—and not Congress—makes the laws. "You mean the president can't lower taxes?" students often say to me in disbelief when they learn otherwise. It is also important for students to understand how the other two branches of government check presidential power. An enduring issue (and one that enters into many election campaigns) is the role of the federal government in relation to the states. For elections prior to the Civil War, I emphasize the importance of the slave clauses in the U.S. Constitution (the Fugitive Slave Clause Article IV Section 2, for example). For elections after the Civil War, I emphasize the importance of the thirteenth, fourteenth, and fifteenth amendments, which ended slavery, ensured equal justice before the law, and enfranchised black males.

Staging an Andrew Jackson vs. Henry Clay Election Debate

It is easy to see why many of these enduring issues are relevant to the election of 1832, which pitted incumbent President Andrew Jackson against Senator Henry Clay. There were fierce rivalries between these two Westerners—both had been candidates in the four-way race of 1824. Textbooks and collections of primary source documents invariably devote major coverage to the Jacksonian period, including Jackson's introduction of the spoils system, the Bank War, Indian Removal, the Tariff of Abominations, and the nullification crisis. In addition, this is the time period when many of the campaign tactics we take for granted today first took root, a legacy of the ever-widening franchise for white males. For all of these reasons I like to set an election debate in this time period.

In the following model of a presidential debate there are seven students on each of two teams, one team arguing that we should reelect President Jackson and the other team backing his opponent, Senator Henry Clay. Each of the seven students on each team is responsible for presenting a speech on one of the subtopics in the first column.

Andrew Jackson vs. Henry Clay, Election of 1832

Subtopic	Issues Raised
The Credentials of Each Candidate: What Makes a Good President?	• How does the prior experience of each candidate equip him to be a good president? • How does the character of each candidate ensure that he will be a good president?
The Bank War	Jackson wants to destroy the Bank of the United States, while Clay wants to preserve it. • It was declared constitutional by the Supreme Court. • What role should the federal government play in regulating the economy and what is the most prudent and fair way to go about it? • Did the bank favor the rich? • Did the bank play politics? • Was the bank beneficial to the economy of the United States?

The Role of the Common Man in Government	Andrew Jackson instituted the spoils system on the federal level beginning in 1828. • Does the spoils system increase the participation of citizens in their government? • Is every person equipped to participate in government? • Does the system lead to patronage and corruption? • Should all government jobs be divorced from politics?
Internal Improvements	What is the proper role of the federal government? • Clay developed the "American System," which promoted spending by the federal government on local projects, whereas Jackson was generally opposed. • Does Clay's "American System" benefit the entire country or merely strengthen the hand of those in power?
Tariff of Abominations and the Nullification Crisis	South Carolina is threatening to nullify the Tariff of Abominations. • Does the tariff benefit the whole nation or only Northern manufacturers? • How would each candidate handle this growing crisis? • Is it better to compromise on the tariff or stand firm on principles of federal power?
Indian Removal Policy	Under Jackson the westward removal of the Cherokee Indians was initiated. Clay opposes it. • Was the policy constitutional? • What would be the consequences of the policy?
Summary Speaker	Andrew Jackson: Man of the people or tyrant? Henry Clay: Friend of the rich and powerful or the Great Compromiser? (Here was a time for each team to restate its important points and to argue for their priority.)

All students in the class read about Jacksonian America in their textbooks, whether they are in the debate, judging the debate, or assigned to a supplementary role such as creating time lines. There is plenty about Jackson's first term in office in any textbook. My job is to fill in information about Henry Clay and to help the debaters locate primary source documents. Collections of relevant documents are easy to locate in Richard Hofstadter's *Great Issues in American History: From the Revolution to the Civil War* (1958), the second volume in his series, which devotes an entire chapter to documents of the Jacksonian Era. In class—before I assign teams—we go over possible arguments on each side of every issue. Once I announce the teams I create a schedule of work due dates and set aside class time for teams to meet as a group. The Summary Speaker acts as group leader because in order to summarize the team's viewpoint, he or she must know what each speaker will say and help the team stay consistent in its arguments. Although team members read and improve one another's first-draft speeches, I also work with each student to elicit the best work possible. In order to stay evenhanded, I never make myself a judge of the debate itself.

Student Speeches

This year when I staged the debate I was pleased to see that the Summary Speakers hit on the essential themes of this election. Jennine, speaking for Jackson, wrote the following as part of her final draft:

> My fellow Americans, we should re-elect President Jackson because for the last four years he has championed your rights, the rights of the common people...One of the reasons the President believes in the rights of common people is because he himself grew up poor...A month before he was born his father died in an accident. When he was thirteen he lost both of his brothers in the Revolutionary War. When fourteen, Jackson's mother died of cholera, leaving him an orphan. Despite all these hardships, he was determined to turn his life around.
>
> What are the ways in which Jackson has benefited the common man? First, he supported the spoils system for the past four years. The spoils sys-

tem gave the President the opportunity to replace old government officials who as Jackson himself said, "are apt to acquire a habit of looking with indifference upon the interests of the public. Office is considered as a form of property, and the government rather as a means of promoting individual interests than as an instrument created solely for the service of the people." Instead he hired his supporters, who supported his ideas and who came from all walks of life. Jackson believes that the common people, no matter what their status, are eligible for a government job.

President Jackson believes the Bank of the United States only benefits the rich. The bank can refrain from giving loans to many people. The Bank gives the rich stocks and loans, which gives them the opportunity to profit. The Bank doesn't give credit to farmers, wage earners and small business-men, making it hard to run their businesses. Andrew Jackson vetoed the creation [*re-chartering*] of the Bank in all of our interests...all of Jackson's vetoes had the country's support. This is why you should vote for Jackson.

Gus, the Summary Speaker for the Clay team gave a very different view of Jackson in this, the first draft of his speech:

Never before has America elected a man with such blatant disregard for his forefathers, and furthermore, the Constitution. He even lied when he became president, by swearing in, when he was not going to uphold the Con-stitution. A liar, a traitor, a murderer, yes, President Jackson has a question-able past. He also has an even more questionable future if we as American voters, reelect him.

My team has shown that President Jackson broke treaties signed by both Americans and Natives. He had no right to do that. He went above the Supreme Court to...kick out the Cherokees from their homeland. Jackson thinks that he is a king. He has brought many friends to power to help rule his presidency. He seems almost like a monarchy though, in the sense that he and his allies rule the entire executive branch.

In addition to his complete and utter power contained in the execu-tive branch, his disregard to the judiciary branch, his power also lies in the legislative branch. This is because Jackson has abused his power to veto bills passed by Congress...

So, ladies and gentlemen of this supposed debate, I can not force you to vote for Clay, but I can strongly advise you, and guarantee you that if Clay gets elected, there will be some changes made around here. Clay is against slavery, and Jackson is for it. Clay is against Indian Removal and Jackson is for it. Jackson is hypocritical, ignorant, a gambler, and a liar who married a bigamist. So, people, when you leave here today, vote for the man with strong views. Vote for Clay!

Jennine addresses her audience in an appropriately inclusive way and shows that Jackson is a "common man" just like us. Our emotions are further moved by her depiction of the difficulties Jackson faced in his youth. She then goes on to give a well-organized defense of Jackson's presidency, highlighting issues in order to show that Jackson worked on our behalf. She demonstrates good reasoning. She uses a very apt quotation from Jackson himself.

Gus also tries to win our emotions. The problem is that he is does not substantiate what he says, so his statements seem hyperbolic. Because I was familiar with the materials he read I knew what he meant when he said, "Jackson is hypocritical, ignorant, a gambler, and a liar who married a bigamist." Jackson had almost no formal education, he did gamble recklessly in his youth, he killed someone in a duel, and he married a woman who thought she was legally divorced from her first husband, which in fact was not yet the case. All of this is fair game and was used during the actual election. But in the revision, Gus needed to refer to facts to substantiate his claims.

While Gus is not expressing his ideas in the first instance very effectively, his thinking is sophisticated. Gus is using what he learned in our study of the U.S. Constitution by referring to the three branches of government and attempting to show how Jackson subverted the founders' plan in order to inflate his own power. My job was to help Gus revise his speech so that he expressed these good ideas more effectively to his audience.

Analyzing and Creating Campaign Paraphernalia

Students love the hoopla campaigns generate through advertisements, cartoons, posters, banners, buttons, and bumper stickers. Once students understand the basic issues of the campaign I set them to work creating these. One bulletin board or wall of the classroom is set aside for each candidate's displays. Who should create these? I usually ask each debater to create one item, but another option is to assign a number of students to each team as publicity agents—especially students with strong artistic skills.

It is fun and instructive to make campaign materials that are authentic to the time period; this fosters the need for further research. A publicity team can be given the task of finding out what to make and producing it. Because what they create will be put to use, motivation is high. I serve the function of prodding them with questions. When do you think the first campaign buttons were made? Students discover that in 1832 campaign ribbons, not buttons, were in use. The ribbons had pictures of the candidate and could be pinned or buttoned onto clothing. Lapel pins and watch fobs with pictures of the candidates were also popular in yesteryear. Now they know what to make. No need for bumper stickers until most Americans drove cars! For an election debate set in the 1920s students can produce campaign songs and radio advertisements with tape recorders, whereas those set after 1950s can include television advertisements made with video cameras.

Political cartooning is historically appropriate to any campaign and this is a great opportunity to teach students how to analyze examples before they create their own cartoons. There are several websites that help students through the process of interpretation (see Appendix F) as well as a useful Cartoon Analysis Worksheet produced by the National Archives (see Figure 6.1 and Appendix J). These help students analyze the techniques that cartoonists use, such as exaggeration, distortion, and the juxtaposition of unexpected elements, and further aid students in deciphering the cartoonist's point of view.

An Exercise in Analyzing Visual Symbolism

In cartoons, visual symbols often represent ideas—a sophisticated concept. Every object and its placement has meaning. I help students make the connection between image and idea by using the well-known iconography of the Statue of Liberty. As students look at a photograph of it, I ask the following questions:

- Why do her face and her clothing look like a Greek statue? (Greece was the "cradle of democracy.")
- Why does she hold a torch in her raised right hand? (She functions as a lighthouse guiding ships.)
- How is she "enlightening" the world, as the title of the statue suggests? (With her torch she beckons newcomers from around the world and welcomes them to the shores of liberty.)
- Why does she wear a crown with seven rays? (She sheds her rays on seven continents and seven seas.)
- Liberty holds a tablet in her left arm on which "July 4

Fig 6.1 Cartoon Analysis Worksheet

THE U.S. NATIONAL ARCHIVES & RECORDS ADMINISTRATION
www.archives.gov   Monday, January 8, 2007

Cartoon Analysis Worksheet

Level 1

Visuals	Words (not all cartoons include words)
1. List the objects or people you see in the cartoon.	1. Identify the cartoon caption and/or title.
	2. Locate three words or phrases used by the cartoonist to identify objects or people within the cartoon.
	3. Record any important dates or numbers that appear in the cartoon.

Level 2

Visuals	Words
2. Which of the objects on your list are symbols? 3. What do you think each symbol means?	4. Which words or phrases in the cartoon appear to be the most significant? Why do you think so? 5. List adjectives that describe the emotions portrayed in the cartoon.

Level 3

A. Describe the action taking place in the cartoon.

B. Explain how the words in the cartoon clarify the symbols.

C. Explain the message of the cartoon.

D. What special interest groups would agree/disagree with the cartoon's message? Why?

Page URL: http://www.archives.gov/education/lessons/worksheets/cartoon.html

The U.S. National Archives and Records Administration
8601 Adelphi Road, College Park, MD 20740-6001 • Telephone: 1-86-NARA-NARA or 1-866-272-6272

1776" is inscribed in Roman numerals. Why this date? What other "tablets" are important in the Bible? (We celebrate the nation's birth on the July 4, 1776, when the Declaration of Independence was written. The Ten Commandments were written on a tablet.)

- At Liberty's feet is a broken chain. What might it symbolize? (Liberty frees the enslaved.)
- What is the overall message of the statue? (In America, liberty reigns and shines her light on the rest of the world.)

BORN TO COMMAND.

OF VETO MEMORY.

HAD I BEEN CONSULTED.

VETO

CONSTITUTION of the UNITED STATES of America

Internal Improvements Bank

KING ANDREW THE FIRST.

Fig 6.2 Comparing the iconography in this cartoon to that used in the Statue of Liberty helps students understand its meaning.

After this exercise, students quickly grasp the iconography of the cartoon in Figure 6.2, "Born to Command: King Andrew the First." As students examine a copy of the cartoon, I ask a similar line of questioning:

• How do we know that Andrew Jackson is being portrayed as a king? (He has a crown, robe, and scepter.)
• Would Jackson want to be viewed as a king? (No, Jackson said he championed the common man and was proud to be one.)
• Along with his scepter he holds a document marked, "veto." Why? (Jackson vetoed more laws passed by Congress than any other president up until his time.)
• What lies beneath Jackson's feet? (Documents including the U.S. Constitution, Internal Improvements, and a book on the U.S. judiciary.)
• Why would the cartoonist portray these things underfoot? (He is trampling on them.)
• What is the overall message of the cartoon? (Jackson is a tyrant who has usurped his presidential powers by excessive use of the veto, ignoring the founding documents of the United States and rulings of the Supreme Court.)

It is fun to compare this cartoon to a pro-Jackson one entitled "Old Jack, the famous New Orleans mouser, clearing Uncle Sam's Barn of Bank and Clay Rats" available online at HarpWeek.com (see Appendix F). Jackson is portrayed here as a cat, the hero of the scene, and on the cat's tail is written "veto." This cartoonist liked Jackson's use of the veto, especially when it came to its effectiveness regarding the bank. Jackson's enemies are portrayed as rats, scurrying away from the powerful "Old Jack" cat. It was typical in this time period to use rats to portray corruption. The party of reform is often symbolized by a broom that sweeps clean the filth from a barn.

It is not easy to create good slogans accompanied by strong visual images, and I am always surprised by how clever students are at creating them. For example, one year the class started making puns on the meaning of the word *clay* with slogans and banners that said, "Vote Clay: Clay will Mold America the Right Way," and, "Vote for Jackson or America Will End Up Like a Lump of Clay." The Clay team created images of the American System with a flag, symbols for financial prosperity (a dollar sign), and images of road and canal building. One student created a drawing of Jackson enclosed in a red circle with "VETO" written across his face (in other words, veto the president's reelection). Another student created a poster using the clever pun, "You Can Bank On Henry Clay."

Staging and Judging the Election Debate

I like to make the debate itself as formal as possible because I want students to understand how strict adherence to rules ensures impartiality. As students grow impassioned, they are tempted to call out; the rules hold them in check, and I don't have to get involved. I simply act as the referee ensuring that no student speaks beyond time allotments: four minutes for constructive speeches and two minutes for rebuttals.

When I started developing election debates for the classroom, I knew nothing about debating. Fortunately, it is easy to order books or look on websites for rules and tips. I never hesitate to adapt these to my own purposes. Our usual format follows the sequence of subtopics listed in the chart on pages 151–152. We begin with the speeches about the credentials of each candidate. The opening speaker for Jackson speaks for up to four minutes, and this is followed immediately by a four-minute speech for Clay. Then I give a timed break (one or two minutes) for these speakers to prepare rebuttals. Speakers then can take up to two minutes to present their rebuttals. Next the students arguing about a different issue take the debate floor, and the speech/rebuttal process is repeated. Sometimes I allow the entire team to get together in order to help the speakers prepare rebuttals

Debate Score Sheet

Topic: [The Bank War] _____

TEAM: [Andrew Jackson] _____ DEBATOR [Marcus Adams] _____

ARGUMENTS:	Did the speaker present convincing, well-reasoned ideas supported by facts?
REBUTTAL:	Did the speaker give a point for point refutation of the opponent's speech, presenting well-reasoned arguments and facts?
PRESENTATION:	Were the constructive and rebuttal speeches delivered in a clear, forceful, and convincing manner? Did the speaker win your trust?
SCORE:	1-5 points with 5 the highest score possible. ___ Constructive Arguments ___ Rebuttal ___ Presentation

Fig 6.3 Debate Score Sheet

Promotional Materials Score Card

TEAM: _____ NAME OF STUDENT _____

A.	Check item produced: ☐ Poster ☐ Flyer ☐ Buttons ☐ Bumper Stickers ☐ Radio or TV Ads ☐ Political Cartoon ☐ Other _____
B.	Score: 1-5 point with 5 the highest score possible. ___ 1. Was the message of the promotional material clear? ___ 2. Did it reflect an understanding of the issues in the campaign? ___ 3. Was it produced with creativity and care? ___ 4. Was it clever and did it carry emotional punch?

Fig 6.4 Promotional Materials Score Card

and sometimes I let them pass notes to one another. The advantage to this is that everyone functions as a team throughout the debate, listening to each speaker carefully and formulating arguments along the way, whether it is their turn to speak or not.

There are many ways to decide who judges the debate. The only thing I stipulate is that judges must evaluate it as if they were living during the time period. Sometimes I give the judges identity cards. For example, a judge who is a banker from the East would definitely be opposed to Jackson's policies on the Bank, whereas a Westerner with little capital would approve. Using this model it is important to set up a group of "swing voters" who enter with no strong feelings for one candidate or the other.

One year another section of eighth-grade American history students acted as our judges. Their teacher was delighted; by listening to my class, her class learned a great deal. I asked each judge to fill out the Debate Score Sheet shown in Figure 6.3 for every speaker in the debate. (Note: While I like to let the campaign paraphernalia simply add to the esprit of the whole event, it is also possible to score each promotional item and add the points gained to each team's overall score). The judges can take notes in the spaces on the sheet. After each pair of speakers has finished, we pause so that the judges can fill in this form. I also fill in a score sheet as I listen for the purpose of my own record keeping. When we are including other election materials in our scoring, we use the Promotional Materials Score Card shown in Figure 6.4. (See also Appendix L.)

When the debate is over I ask each judge to submit a list of how many points each team earned. I collect their tabulations and add them up to figure out which team won the debate. I learned the hard way not to let students know their individual scores. Some students brag when they find they earned top scores from the judges, even if their team lost the debate! In some years students teased team members who scored poorly, blaming them for their group's defeat. Because I want to build team spirit and cooperation, I insist that teams win or lose as a whole unit. However, I do write each student a personal note giving him or her my own appraisal of how well he or she performed, and return the rubrics form found at the end of this chapter.

Announcing which side won is always suspenseful. The debate (like an election itself) is an inherently competitive format. Students want to know immediately who was "elected." Some years the losing team takes their defeat very hard indeed. I remember Jocelyn whining, "What was the point of working so hard if we lost?" This is an important teachable moment, and I stop and ask students to reflect on the point of the activity. "Did you all learn a lot?" I ask, and invariably the answer is, "Yes." Then I assure them that this was the ultimate goal of the activity. After a few rancorous endings to the debates, I learned not to let things go bitter; I sweeten the announcement by distributing pieces of a "liberty cake" and some punch. There is also a larger message here to stress with students. In a democracy the losing side accepts defeat and joins the winners to work together to make a better country—or so it should be.

Follow-up Activities

Interpreting History and Ranking Presidents

Of the six or seven times I have held a Jackson versus Clay election debate, Clay won more often than not. At first this surprised me, because Andrew Jackson is portrayed as laudable in the typical American textbook. Yet once students get immersed in the issues, it is not hard to understand Clay's appeal. We no longer admire Andrew Jackson's career as Indian fighter, and his Indian Removal policy is regarded as one of the great blights of our past. There *were* voices opposing the policy even then, including Henry Clay's. Clay was no advocate of abolition, but he was a leader of the American Colonization Society (which advocated funding the return of Africans to Africa). This is more than one can say for Jackson, who remained silent on the issue. The demise of the Bank of America led to the panic of 1837, and today we recognize the need for federal regulation of the economy. It is also interesting for students to note that Lincoln began his political career as a Whig and great admirer of Henry Clay. By taking opposing eyewitness viewpoints set during past elections, students begin to become interested in historical interpretation itself. How and why do the reputations of past presidents rise and fall? On what basis do we judge them? How do current events change our perspective on past events? Students enjoy reading about how various historians judge a president's performance and about how our evaluation of past presidents has changed over time.

After staging an election, it is fun for students to rank the presidents as they learn about them in their textbooks. By now they should have a sharpened set of criteria by which to judge a president's record. Clinton Rossiter, in his famous book *The American Presidency* ([1956] 1987), ranks his top choices as follows: Washington, Lincoln, Wilson, Jackson, Theodore Roosevelt, Jefferson, Franklin D. Roosevelt, and Truman. Do students agree with his ranking? Why or why not? And how would students put more recent presidents such as Ronald Reagan on their list? Students enjoy interviewing parents and grandparents about whom they voted for in past elections and whether their opinion of a past president has changed over time. How do students think the current president will rank, and why?

Designing a Monument or Currency

In a review of *Andrew Jackson: His Life and Times* (2005), by H. W. Brands, Ted Widmer wrote in *The Washington Post*,

> *Jackson, after all, occupies a peculiar place in the Hall of Dead Presidents. We see him every day on the $20 bill and hear of him in*

the overused phrase 'Jacksonian democracy,' but we do not know him nearly as well as we do most of his predecessors or the great president who learned from him, Abraham Lincoln. There is no Jackson Memorial—only an equestrian statue facing the White House, somewhat menacingly. (2005, BW05)

This comment suggests an interesting activity: Ask students to design a fitting monument to President Jackson. What images or words would it contain? Where in Washington, D.C., would they place the monument? For twentieth-century elections, students can debate whether or not we should honor presidents such as Woodrow Wilson or Ronald Reagan with a memorial or coin and, if so, design them.

Studying the Losers

And what about the great losers of presidential elections? Men like Henry Clay and William Jennings Bryan deserve to be studied in their own right. They contributed to American history over many more years than the term of any one president. You will find students fascinated to follow their careers even though they did not win. By holding a "What if?" discussion (What if Henry Clay had won?), students gain fresh insights into American history. Students can also compare the careers of presidents after they leave office. Interesting cases are John Quincy Adams, who returned to government as a congressman, and Jimmy Carter, who has carved a significant role for himself as a peacemaker.

Role-Playing a Cabinet Meeting

Finally, another engaging election follow-up activity is to ask students to role-play cabinet meetings of the newly-elected president as he (and one day *she*) confronts difficult decisions and seeks advice. (See Appendix F for materials published by Interact based on this idea.) If you live near any of the presidential libraries, by all means visit them; some of these libraries help students stage cabinet meetings using primary source documents in their holdings. After the role-play, students can compare a president's campaign promises to his or her actual service in office and evaluate whether or not the candidate responded well to the exigencies of the day.

Assessment

Restaging an election debate is the most purely political of the eyewitness strategies presented in this book. The activity presumes that students know something about how their government works. Its focus is leadership and laws. Yet in some ways it feels closest to home because elections are recurring events in the lives of students themselves.

No given election exists in a vacuum. My experience is that students instinctively grasp the interconnectedness of politics and the lives of ordinary citizens, especially when experiencing American history from the eyewitness viewpoint. For example, because I preceded a Jacksonian election debate with an eyewitness travelogue, my students felt they knew this country of ours intimately. Supporters of Clay could speak from "personal experience" about the need to build turnpikes and canals at federal expense because *they had traveled by these means themselves.* Presidential candidates often tour the country to learn about regional issues so that they can better represent all of us.

The election debate is also extremely useful for comparing different time periods in American history. If groups of students stage different campaigns set in different time periods throughout the year, there are many things to compare and contrast, including how we elect our presidents, the qualities of good leadership, what political parties have stood for over time, and what issues are important to Americans and why.

Rubrics for Speeches

Topic	Criteria	Mark from 1–5
Rhetoric	Did you establish yourself as someone whose opinions we trust? Did you win our emotions? Did you reason effectively? Did you substantiate your claims with facts?	
Presentation	Did you speak with purpose and poise? Did you project your voice?	
Rebuttal	Did you listen to your opponent carefully? Did you respond to his/her arguments point for point? Did you present relevant facts?	
Collaborative Team Effort	Did you cooperate with teammates? Did you help devise team strategy?	
Promotional Materials (if assigned)	Did you create colorful and well-executed campaign material? Did you convey the message of your team effectively?	
Overall Comment		

Chapter Seven

Scrapbooks: Documenting the Past Across Time

I invented a scrapbook—and if I do say it myself, it was the only rational scrapbook the world has ever seen.

Mark Twain, c. 1906

Scrapbooks are collections of documents that preserve information. Sometimes the collector has a passion for saving items related to a particular topic of interest. Most often we associate scrapbooks with family record-keeping. In these cases scrapbooks hold personal artifacts such as wedding invitations, birth announcements, travel memorabilia, and obituaries interspersed with news clippings about historical events that affected the family. Scrapbooks therefore form a narrative that places the personal within the context of social and political change. According to Danielle Bias, Rebecca Black, and Susan Tucker (who maintains a website at Tulane University on scrapbooks; see Appendix G), "We think of the scrapbook and the album as part of an individual response to photography, printing, and the desire to document oneself. Creating one's own Web page, for example, is very much in the same tradition as scrapbook-making." We now use digital photographs, cull images from the Internet, and collect and paste images on personal Web pages. Perhaps as a counterreaction to this technological onslaught, devotees of the old-fashioned album are reviving scrapbooking as an art and craft. A recent spate of how-to books attests to this trend.

In the classroom, however, it is recent technology that makes scrapbooking such an appealing project to explore with students. Only in the past few years have I experimented with its endless variations. For example, students can create their own scrapbooks from the point of view of a character they create or a historical person they research. Web quests become the means by which students acquire the documents they will cut and paste into their scrapbooks and the means by which they find models upon which they can base their own "documents." Students can collect and present images and documents in digital scrapbooks using such programs as PowerPoint, or they can burn their own CDs, but I prefer that images and documents be downloaded and cut and pasted onto paper—the medium in which scrapbooks first developed.

As an eyewitness strategy, scrapbooks belong at the end of this book for a number of reasons. The form did not develop until the nineteenth century, so I wait until I reach the Civil War era or beyond to give this assignment. Also, because scrapbooks are themselves a compendium of documents, I use the assignment only after students are adept at analyzing a variety of types of primary sources.

Scholars trace the origins of the scrapbook to the sixteenth century commonplace book in which people collected proverbs and sayings for the purpose of reflecting on them. The advent of the scrapbook as we know it began in the mid-nineteenth century along with rapid technological advances in both printing and photography. Why throw out all those colorful advertisements, valentines, postcards, labels, visiting cards, and ticket stubs that came one's way when they could be saved instead? Now, as then, it is photographs that people most want to preserve. According to Susan Tucker's website, photographic albums were first advertised nationwide in 1860 in *Harper's Weekly*. By 1872 Mark Twain had patented his scrapbook, the only invention on which he ever made money. According to the PBS website about Twain and his invention:

Mark Twain was a lifelong creator and keeper of scrapbooks. He took them with him everywhere and filled them with souvenirs, pictures, and articles about his books and performances. But in time, he grew tired of the lost glue, rock-hard paste, and the swearing that resulted from the standard scrapbook process. So, he came up with the idea of printing thin strips of glue on the pages to make updates neat and easy to do. In 1872, he patented his "self-pasting" scrapbook, and by 1901, at least 57 different types of his albums were available. (PBS)

The fact that this invention was so successful at the turn of the last century points to the popular nature of the pastime.

Scrutinizing Scrapbooks

Even when scrapbooks go on display in museums visitors are not allowed to turn the pages. The best way for students to see examples of scrapbooks is to look in family attics and query grandparents. Sometimes family albums can be found at rummage sales. Fortunately, there are a number of websites that include digitized images of pages from scrapbooks. Students can view these online exhibits and make deductions about them. Who collected the items and why? What do they reflect about the collector's life, interests, and the time period in which he or she lived? I recommend looking at scrapbooks on Susan Tucker's website at Tulane University, as well as pages from Mark Twain's scrapbooks on PBS (see Appendix G). A website at the University of Delaware titled "Self Works" divides its exhibit into examples from men's and women's scrapbooks, inviting an interesting discussion of gender roles. Because greater career opportunities were open to men, they were more likely to document their professional accomplishments, as did Mark Twain, whereas women's scrapbooks were often related to family or social life. Feminist scholars have demonstrated how seemingly inconsequential documents like scrapbooks can be important sources of information about the American past. The curator of the Florence Reynolds (1879–1949) scrapbook online at the University of Delaware comments,

Reynolds was graduated from the Lewis Institute in Chicago in 1901, after which she spent the summer and fall visiting relatives in

Salt Lake City, Utah. The scrapbook she kept from that period includes clippings, invitations, theater programs, correspondence, game cards for social events, personal calling cards, and photographs. The ephemera and memorabilia saved by Miss Reynolds provides colorful documentation of social conventions and customs of upper middle-class society at the turn of the century. (Melvin)

The American Memory website of the Library of Congress includes the scrapbooks kept from 1897 to 1911 by Elizabeth Smith Miller and her daughter Anne Fitzhugh Miller. They are filled with news articles, photographs, and programs related to their work in the women's suffrage movement. According to the website, "They offer a unique look at the political and social atmosphere of the time as well as chronicle the efforts of two women who were major participants in the suffrage movement" (American Memory).

Variations on the Scrapbook Assignment

Like other eyewitness projects, students incorporate events into their scrapbooks as they learn about them in their textbooks and complete independent research. They bring a period to life by highlighting the everyday context of historical events. Asking students to create a scrapbook for a historical person or family provides a good means to study the causes and effects of social change over generations.

I have worked with two models for the scrapbooking strategy. In the first, students work in groups to create a family saga over several generations. The family is fictional, and the students create a story line that reflects the time period they are documenting. Each member of the group develops the role of one person in the kinship network. For example, when my students make scrapbooks of an immigrant family from 1890 to 1930, their composite effort reflects life in the old country compared to life in America. Photographs of successively owned houses, clothing, horses, and cars attest to the increasing upward mobility and Americanization of each generation. Documents they paste into their albums include passports, applications for citizenship, newspaper clippings, high school diplomas, letters, and photographs. Their scrapbooks demonstrate the effect of U.S. immigration laws on the fate of family members and reflect the difficulties faced by immigrant groups because of their ethnic, racial, or religious affiliation at different times in our history. Scrapbooks such as these also reflect the accomplishments and contributions of immigrant groups to America.

Another effective time frame for this assignment is 1940 to 1975. In this case the parents' generation would have lived through and fought in World War II while the younger generation grows increasingly conflicted over service in the Vietnam War. The lives of mother and daughter would demonstrate the changing roles of women in American society during World War II and beyond. In "Doing the Decades: Group Investigations in Twentieth Century U. S. History" on the Learning Page of the American Memory website, William R. Fernekes and Harlene Rosenberg suggest ways in which a scrapbook assignment can be adapted for numerous topics of twentieth-century history.

This chapter describes a different model, one in which students create a scrapbook of the life and times of historical figures, in this case African Americans in the Reconstruction era. Because it is unlikely that students could find out all about their real-life subject's ancestors and offspring, this is not a family album. Students delve into one life, and they work individually to document it. First they read about their assigned person and what he or she accomplished, then they search for documents that reflect the time period and events through which he or she lived. The structure of the assignment is infinitely adaptable to other eras.

Making it Fun to Analyze Official Documents

The scrapbooks that students create are compendiums of personal memorabilia and legal documents. Because my classes already have extensive experience analyzing letters, diaries, and other similar documents for the eyewitness strategies, in this unit I focus my teaching on legal documents. These official documents, however, make for very dull reading. The question is how to engage students in the process of teasing out all the fascinating things they can tell us.

I have found one surefire way: I choose documents related to my own life and create an exercise to analyze them. This way I can model how to make sense out of official documents before students go searching for them on their own. Students are very curious to know more about the real lives of their teachers beyond what they see in school, and they are therefore eager to play detective. So if you are willing to share just a bit about your past, your students will be ready to learn all they can.

In combing through my files I found a group of documents issued between 1968 and 1978. These included:

- United States passport issued in 1968
- Certificate of birth for my daughter from 1978
- Certificate of completion of jury duty from 1976
- College diploma from 1969
- New York State Permanent Teaching Certificate from 1971
- Lease for an apartment in 1970
- New York City school license from 1971
- Teaching contract from a school for the 1971–1972 school year

With students in small groups, I distribute one of these items apiece to each group along with a Document Analysis Worksheet (see Figure 7.1).

After each group has filled out their analysis worksheet, they report their findings to the whole class. We start a time line on the board as we discuss the groups' findings. Not until then do we have the chance to put the documents in chronological order. From my passport students can figure out the year I was born, that I am an American citizen, and that my parents' address in New York City was at that time my legal residence. From the photograph in the passport they get to see what I looked like at

Document Analysis Worksheet

Your Name _____ Title of Document _____

A. Is your document (check one)
   ☐ Issued by a governmental agency?
   ☐ Issued by a private organization?
   ☐ A contract between two private citizens?

   How do you know? Explain:_____

B. When was it issued? _____
   To whom was it issued? _____
   By whom was it issued? _____

C. Are there any seals on the document, and what do they tell us?

D. Are there any signatures on the document, and if so what do they tell us?

E. To what does the certificate or legal document attest or certify?

F. Why might it be important for the agency or person who issued this document to retain such a record?

G. Why might it be important for the recipient to keep a copy?

H. What can we learn about the recipient's life from this document?

I. What can we learn about this time period in history from this document?

Fig 7.1 Document Analysis Worksheet

age twenty-one, and I brace myself for the ensuing giggles. From the port of entry stamps they know which countries I visited. Because my college diploma was granted a year after the passport, students correctly deduce that I made this trip the summer before I graduated from college. I signed a lease for an apartment for $150 a month after graduating from college, and it can be presumed that I no longer lived with my parents. I signed the lease in the name "Joan Brodsky," not "Joan Brodsky Schur," leading students to the conclusion that I was not yet married. My rent seems incredibly low by today's standards until students realize that my first teaching job paid only $6,000 a year. Proportionately, my rent was not so low after all! I earned both a state and city license to teach junior high and high school English by the time I was hired for that job. In August of 1976 I completed jury duty, presumably to avoid doing so during the school year. By the time my daughter was born in 1978, I was residing at a third address in New York City, and students assume I was then living with my husband, whose name appears on her birth certificate.

There are also plenty of things students cannot figure out from these documents. What did I do from 1969 until 1971 and how did I support myself? Did I earn any other degrees? When did I get married? We discuss what types of documents would provide such information: a marriage license, a contract, or a diploma. We also discuss why I kept the documents I did. For example, jury duty is a legal obligation and I wanted to save proof that I had fulfilled my responsibilities. My passport was long expired so perhaps I just kept it for sentimental reasons. What other types of legal documents might people save? The class brainstorms a list that includes such items as draft records, income tax returns, wills, bills of sale, deeds, honors, and prizes.

Now I distribute some personal artifacts rather than official documents. These might include postcards mailed home during my trip, birthday cards signed by a grandmother and sister, a playbill for a Broadway show, and a few photos of myself dressed in 60s fashion. The class adds information culled from these items to the time line about my life. The postcard tells us not only that I went to England, but that I visited Stonehenge while there. The content of the postcard attests to my love of history, even then. Students now know I had a living grandmother at age twenty-one and at least one sibling.

Next, using the book *The Timetables of American History* (Urdang 2001), we look up some of the key events in U.S. history for the years 1968 through 1978. We also look up notable events in the arts and science and technology. For most of these years the Vietnam War was raging and the women's rights movement was in full swing. In 1968 Dr. King was assassinated. In 1973 Nixon faced impeachment and resigned from the White House. By 1975 the United States had withdrawn troops from Vietnam, and in 1976 Jimmy Carter was elected president. Naturally, students are interested to know how these events affected my life and people close to me. Did I know or lose anyone who fought in Vietnam? Did I go on any peace marches? Was I at Woodstock? I do not share personal details beyond the artifacts because I want my students to play historian and extract what they can from these primary sources.

I point out that although I never kept a scrapbook during these years, we have in effect created one. The class can see that by looking at an assortment of documents and memorabilia, both official and personal, they can begin to piece together my life within its historical context. I also ask students quickly to make a list of ten things they would put in a scrapbook about their eighth-grade year. We discuss how a person's interests, personal relationships, hobbies, and even political point of view are reflected in the things they choose to save.

Assigning a Reconstruction Scrapbook

The scrapbook assignment I describe here begins in the middle of the Civil War and ends in 1877 with the close of Reconstruction. I find the Reconstruction period difficult to teach. Students find much of it challenging to understand, especially why the status of the Southern states vis-a-vis the federal government kept changing. It can also be an emotional letdown after the high-minded glory of the Civil War. In this assignment each student documents the real-life story of one African American who lived through these years. The era takes on meaning because we personalize the past. As a consequence, an array of African American contributions to American life can be more deeply understood and celebrated.

One reason I choose this transitional time period is to emphasize what it meant to go from slavery to freedom. My class always reads *Narrative of the Life of Frederick Douglass* ([1845] 2003) earlier in the year, so students understand the emotional and physical oppression of slavery. Now I want students to think about how a change in legal status, from slave to free person, would be reflected in documents about any given individual. For example, slaves had no legal last names, their birth dates were not recorded, nor could they marry because the law did not recognize their right to their own offspring. Slaves might be listed by first name in census records or deeds. In this light it is moving to look at marriage certificates recorded by the Freedman's Bureau, established by an act of Congress in 1865. The federal government now regarded former slaves as people with legal rights; their last names were recorded because their families were legally recognized. I also want students to appreciate the ways African Americans contributed to the war effort and Reconstruction and to think about what the withdrawal of federal troops would portend for African Americans in the South after 1877. I tell students that the essential questions we will try to answer at the end of the scrapbook project are:

- What difficulties did African Americans face during this time period?
- What were the different strategies they adopted to overcome setbacks?
- What did African Americans accomplish during this time period?

Locating Subjects for the Study

I did the initial research to find historical figures for students to research. Several PBS websites were especially useful, including those for the programs *Africans in America*, *The Rise and Fall of Jim Crow*, *Reconstruction: The Second Civil War*, and *This Far By Faith*. Also of help were the Digital Schomburg collection entitled "African American Women Writers of the Nineteenth Century" and the book *Black Saga: The African American Experience: A Chronology* by Charles M. Christian. Details on all of these sources can be found in Appendix G. The list of African Americans that I developed ranges from the famous to the obscure and includes leaders such as Frederick Douglass, Booker T. Washington, Harriet Tubman, and Sojourner Truth; people elected to Congress such as Blanche K. Bruce and

Elliot R. Revels; teachers and leaders of educational institutions, including Sarah Thompson (wife of Henry Highland Garnet) and Susie King Taylor; and religious leaders such as Fannie Jackson and Daniel L. Payne. Also on the list were several African Americans who won the Congressional Medal of Honor for fighting in the Civil War.

I looked for equal numbers of males and females, including abolitionists, doctors, lawyers, and writers, and I found people of interest in all categories. Some were born free but most were born slaves. Photographs were available for almost all of them in formal Victorian attire. When we posted the photos in our classroom, it was evident that this was a very distinguished group of Americans, even if some are currently not well known. In class I described some individuals on the list as "unknown," and Max, an African American student, corrected me, blurting out, "You mean they are unsung heroes." I quickly agreed that he was right. All students in the class felt proud to undertake this assignment. But Max and another African American student were especially so. Max wanted to be Sergeant William H. Carney, who fought with the 54th Massachusetts and won a Congressional Medal of Honor, and Tyler chose John Jones, a wealthy abolitionist and supporter of John Brown. Some of the people on the list are so famous that students had no trouble locating documents about their lives. Gen made a scrapbook as Frederick Douglass and found an entire collection devoted to him at the American Memory website. Obscure documents about the Douglass family were also available, such as the regimental records of his two sons who fought with the Union.

Finding Documents to Support the Study

The cast of characters I chose initially did not work out as perfectly as I had hoped, because only some subjects on the list were active throughout the Reconstruction era. For example, Susie King Taylor worked as a nurse during the Civil War and founded a private school in the South in the early years of Reconstruction. Eventually she moved North, where the only work she found was as a domestic servant. William H. Carney ended up working for the U.S. Postal Service in Massachusetts. These facts do tell us important things about the opportunities open to African Americans in this time period, but they do not tell my students a lot about Reconstruction.

Nonetheless, the subjects of their scrapbooks did live through the era and as long as students keep collecting documents *related* to the time period and inferring to the best of their abilities how their character *would have* felt about them, the scrapbook assignment remains a success. The challenge I want each student to face is this: How can I convey the facts I *do* know about my person through the documents I collect?

One way to substitute person-specific documents for ones that represent both the person and the era is to look for generic documents. For example, for those African Americans on our list who fought in the Civil War, one such document might be a recruiting poster issued by the War Department just after the Emancipation Proclamation. Blanche K. Bruce, a senator from Mississippi, might have kept photographs of sharecroppers in his state, so I told Noah to go in search of those. Elizabeth Hobbs Keckley, the seamstress for Mary Todd Lincoln, might have treasured photographs of the First Lady in dresses she had tailored for her. When I suggested to Rebecca that she go in search of photos of Mary Todd Lincoln in her regalia, she was thrilled. Alexander T. Augusta, the first black surgeon in the Union Army and later faculty member of Howard University, might have collected photographs of soldiers whose lives he saved, advertisements of medical equipment he wished to purchase, or his diploma from Trinity Medical College in Toronto where he earned his degree. Thinking like this is where the fun comes in, and students eventually get into the swing of it.

Another tack to take is to make facsimile documents of ones that surely did exist. Ally suggested this approach to me before I mentioned it to the class. She researched Sarah Parker Remond, an abolitionist from New England, who toured England giving antislavery speeches. Ally wanted to know if she could make Remond's passport and put it in her scrapbook. I said, "Let's see what you can find out about passports issued during this time period. Once you do, go ahead." This approach opens up another possibility for using documents such as birth, death, and marriage certificates: finding models and then changing how they are filled out. After Gen downloaded the military records of the Douglass sons, we could use those as model forms for other African American soldiers.

It is worth discussing with students the importance of authenticity, even while allowing them a little leeway. Programs like FireWorks enable students to change, combine, and otherwise tamper with downloaded images. While these programs can be useful tools, students need to be aware of the misuse of these technologies in falsifying facts. Another way to help students sort out fact from its embellishment is to carefully watch a PBS or History Channel documentary. We might be looking at a photograph of Frederick Douglass and then a slave cabin *like* the one he grew up in, but not his *actual* cabin. Documentaries rarely clarify this issue. When do these substitutions further our understanding of history, and when do they distort history? This is a question worthy of discussion as students bring creativity to their scrapbooks.

Instructions for Students

After students are assigned roles, they can get to work. How fancy their scrapbooks become depends on you and the time you want students to spend on them. The first year I used this eyewitness strategy, I opted for a very simple format: sheets of eleven-by-seventeen-inch construction paper folded in two and stapled in the middle. Details of a scrapbook assignment follow.

General Guidelines

1. Create a cover for your scrapbook. Include a title and a visual image such as a photograph of your assigned person.
2. Create an introductory page in your scrapbook. Include a copy of the Emancipation Proclamation on the introductory page with a handwritten comment about what it means to "you."
3. Create one page for each year from 1863 to 1877 plus a concluding page.
4. On the back of each page, make a time line of important events that happened in that year in the United States. Add in dates gradually as you read your textbook and we study events in class.
5. Include a handwritten explanation for everything you paste into your scrapbook that tells what it is and what it means "to you." Each document should be placed in chronological order. Things preceding the Civil War can be placed on the introductory page.
6. For every item you include, fill out the appropriate Document

Analysis Worksheet from the National Archives website (e.g., written document, photo, cartoon, map, artifact, etc.). You can download these and fill them out by hand or fill them in directly on the website and then print them out.

7. Make a bibliography of the websites you used for every document.
8. At the very end, write an obituary or eulogy for your person.

Facts to Highlight

Locate two to three websites about your person. Bookmark these and print out relevant information.

In the biographies you read, single out *three important facts* that are essential to understanding what your person accomplished in life. If possible, space these out so as to include something accomplished before the Civil War, during the Civil War, and after the Civil War. Then think about what kind of document you could find to illustrate those accomplishments. Fill out the planning chart.

Planning Chart

Fact to Highlight	Type of Document to Display

Documents to Include

Individualized Document

Start researching the Web to see if you can find primary sources written by or about your person. Assuming you cannot find these, search the Web to find documents on which to model a facsimile document. (For example, what does a diploma look like from a certain college? A teacher's certificate?) Fill in a Document Analysis Worksheet for each document you use, list it on your bibliography, and paste the document into your scrapbook with a handwritten comment.

Then find one document in each of the following categories and do the same thing.

Last Years of the Civil War

Find a document related to an event at the end of the Civil War, such as Sherman's March, Appomattox, or Lincoln's assassination. Writing in your persona, explain what the event means to you and why you are memorializing this event in your scrapbook.

The Freedman's Bureau (Bureau of Refugees, Freedmen, and Abandoned Lands)

Find a document relevant to the work of the Freedman's Bureau, founded by Congress in 1865 and abolished in 1872. Explain how it would have affected your life or those you know. For example, the bureau issued marriage certificates and created schools. In your handwritten comment explain why you wanted this document in "your" scrapbook.

Legal and Extralegal Discrimination and Intimidation

Find a document that explains or relates to one way in which the rights of African Americans were curtailed in these years, such as:

- Black Codes passed by many former Confederate states at the end of the Civil War.
- The purpose and strategies of the Ku Klux Klan, first organized in Tennessee at the end of the Civil War.
- Race riots, such as those in Memphis and New Orleans in 1866 or Vicksburg in 1875.
- Voting restrictions passed by Southern states, whose purpose it was to deprive African Americans of their right to vote.

Place the document related to the way "your" rights were curtailed on its proper chronological page in your scrapbook, and in your handwritten notes, explain how these acts have affected "you" and/or what you did to combat them.

Sharecropping

Find a document that relates to the sharecropping system and exemplifies in some way how it functioned. One such document might be a contract between a landowner and sharecropper. Explain why you are including it in your scrapbook.

Material Culture

Include an advertisement, label, or photograph for clothing, appliances, furniture, or tools from the period. Relate what you have chosen to "your" life and show why it is important to you.

Choose One Topic from the Following List

From the list below choose the *one* topic that has most relevance to "your" life. Find two documents that relate to that topic, and in your scrapbook explain what they mean to you.

- The founding of schools and colleges by and for African Americans such as Morehouse, Fisk, and Spelman
- The role of religion in African American life, such as the work of the African Methodist Episcopal Church (est. 1816) or the Colored Methodist Episcopal Church (est. 1870)
- Contributions of African Americans to the arts and sciences, including music, literature, and scientific or technological advances
- African Americans in state and federal government, their roles, how they won them, what they accomplished, and when and how they lost them
- African Americans and Africa, the ongoing work of missionaries, foreign ministers, and those who settled in Africa

(For an African American scrapbook extending up to 1900, I would suggest adding topics such as Jim Crow laws, the founding of various organizations and publications to further civil rights, and the migration North, etc.)

Types of Documents To Look For

Keep track of the documents you find and try to collect a variety of different types. For each one you find, check it off the list.

Official or legal documents

___Death certificate

___Certificate of marriage

___Diploma

___Purchase of sale

___Lease

___Award

___Military record (draft, discharge, etc.)

___ Income tax returns

___ Will

___ Deed

___ Inventory

___ Church or other religious records

___ Patent

___ Census report

___ Congressional report

___ Passport

___ Other

Printed documents

___ Newspaper and magazine articles

___ Cards (greeting cards, visiting cards, dance cards, etc.)

___ Advertisements

___ Labels

___ Photographs

___ Maps

___ Tickets

___ Brochures

___ Telegrams

___ Publications (book, pamphlet, etc.)

___ Other

Handwritten documents

___ Correspondence

___ Diaries

___ Notes

___ Drawings

___ Handwritten drafts of publications

___ Other

Facilitating Student Work

Whenever I plan an eyewitness assignment I consult the textbook to make sure I am incorporating most of the information students will need to know. For the Reconstruction scrapbook, I chose topics, such as the establishment of the Freedman's Bureau, that students would find easiest to understand when reading the textbook on their own. This enables them to do some reading, note taking, and Web searching on their own while I teach the more complicated content in class, such as the impeachment trial of Andrew Johnson and Congressional Reconstruction. I also make sure to cover some material on black cultural life not typically covered in textbooks, such as the role of religion.

When assigning roles I reserve the African American congressmen for students who are able to work more independently. Their lives would not make much sense without an understanding of Congressional Reconstruction, so I tell those students to read ahead in the text. Because students use the back of each page in their scrapbooks as a time line, they can start to situate an individual's life within its historical context.

To facilitate student Web searches, I post a list of useful URLs for students on our class website, including a variety of time lines of the period. Getting started is not easy; students expect instant results whereas I want them to get a taste for the patience historians need to locate historic records and make sense of them. The frustration some students experience eases, however, when I take the entire class to the computer lab to look for documents. When students have their eureka moments, they call me over excitedly, and I stop the class to announce the find. Everyone grows excited and more determined to find things of interest.

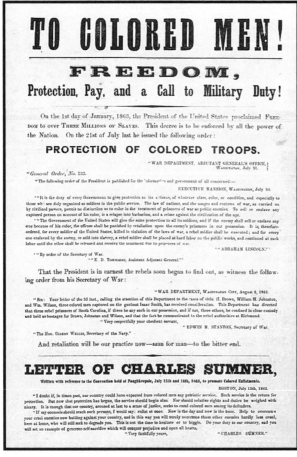

Fig 7.2 This poster, like the one that Max found for his scrapbook, sheds light on what motivated African Americans to fight in the Civil War.

In fact, one year students found more documents pertaining to the people they studied than even I expected. For example, Noah found documents signed by Blanche K. Bruce for sale at a site that markets historical documents. Next to these in his scrapbook, Noah wrote, "These are two of the documents I signed as Recorder of Deeds for the District of Columbia." Rebecca was excited when she found the cover page of Elizabeth Hobbs Keckley's book *Behind the Scenes or Thirty Years a Slave and Four Years in the White House.* In her scrapbook she wrote the following caption:

This is a book I wrote about my experiences in the White House as a seamstress. Since the recent publication I have lost many friends. They think I am a traitor because I dished up the gossip about everything.

I was not expecting Tyler to come up with a primary source about wealthy abolitionist John Jones, yet he found his Certificate of Freedom from 1844 posted online by the Chicago Historical Society. It was issued by a judge of the Circuit Court of Madison, Illinois, and testified that John Jones was "a free person of color, a resident or citizen of the state of Illinois and entitled to be respected accordingly, in Person and Property at all times and places." Tyler's caption for this moving document lacked any personal connection to it, however, reading only, "A document granting emancipation to John Jones."

Max studied William Harvey Carney, who fought with the 54th

Massachusetts regiment. He found a recruiting poster at the site of the Massachusetts Historical Society that read, "Now in Camp at Readville! 54th Regiment! Mass. Volunteers of African Descent. Col. Robert G. Shaw. Colored Men, Rally Round the Flag of Freedom! Bounty $100 at the Expiration of the Term of Service. Pay, $13.00 Month."

In his caption Max wrote, "Two of Frederick Douglass' sons were also in the 54th with me." Although brief, this caption is personal, and he is using what he has learned in class by listening to other students. He knew about the Douglass sons from Gen, who was doing a scrapbook on Frederick Douglass himself.

As a class we also made another connection to the 54th Massachusetts regiment; "class member" Charles Lenox Remond was a recruiting agent for the 54th. Times like these are when things get really exciting for students; they put together what they have learned from discrete documents to reconstruct a larger picture of the past.

By sharing information as we went along, the entire class gained greater insight into the African American community at this time in history. But I realized that students needed help expanding their captions into more complete statements. I took a two-pronged approach to this. I brainstormed with students what their personal connections might have been to the documents they found, and we spent more time analyzing and comparing documents as a class. For example, perhaps Carney saw a recruiting poster like this one and it encouraged him to sign up. What might have made him do so? This is where the Document Analysis Worksheets are useful. They tell me how carefully students are analyzing primary sources and how I can help them make more inferences based on what they find. For example, Max's Poster Analysis Worksheet showed that he understood that the purpose of the poster was "to supply the army with troops." But he did not investigate what this meant to "colored men."

Rather than work just with Max, however, I chose this opportunity to compare two documents with the entire class. One was the document Max found, "Rally Round the Flag of Freedom," which appears in Budge Weidman's lesson on the website of the National Archives. I located the second document, a recruitment poster from Rhode Island, from the New-York Historical Society.

Fig 7.3 Old posters are documents that reveal the tenor of the times and make for valuable documents in student scrapbooks.

We do not know if the Rhode Island poster was issued before or after the Emancipation Proclamation, which changed the purpose of the war. The Rhode Island poster appeals to white soldiers to fight, and its message is quite clear: The war is being fought to protect the Constitution and preserve the Union. We know, on the other hand, that the poster Max found was created after Lincoln issued the Emancipation Proclamation in 1863, because only then did the Union army recruit black soldiers. A quotation on the poster from Charles Sumner reads, "Set an example of generous self-sacrifice which will conquer prejudice and open all hearts." A quotation from Lincoln attempts to allay fears about the treatment of black prisoners of war at the hands of Confederates. The appeal is not to preserve the Union, but rather the cause of freedom. The hopes and fears of African Americans thus come to life by juxtaposing the two posters. Their fight for freedom was very real; because they fought in the war, they extended the meaning of freedom for all Americans. After our class discussion of the two posters, Max went back and added on to his brief caption:

> After Lincoln issued the Emancipation Proclamation I was heartened to see posters like this one recruiting men of color. This is what I had been waiting for, a chance to fight for freedom. I went immediately to the recruiting office in New Bedford where I enlisted on the spot.

Students found many creative ways to incorporate photographs into their scrapbooks. The student who studied nurse and teacher Susie King Taylor found a period photograph of Savannah, Georgia, which she labeled, "My hometown." She also downloaded the frontispiece for a facsimile edition of *The Freedman's Spelling-Book* (Ayers 2003–2006) and photographs of African American children standing outside of their new schools like the one she founded in the South. Noah, working on Blanche K. Bruce, located the marriage rules issued by the Freedman's Bureau in 1865. He pasted them into his scrapbook opposite a racist cartoon that demonstrates the way many white Southern Democrats viewed the organization: "The Freedman's Bureau! An Agency to Keep the Negro in Idleness at the Expense of the White Man. Twice vetoed by the President, and made a law by Congress. Support Congress & you support the Negro. Sustain the President and you protect the White man." (This cartoon can be found at the "American Political Prints" section of HarpWeek.com; see References.) These primary sources, especially when looked at in tandem, bring the period to life in a visceral way. In the end I am grateful to my students who have brought to light many fascinating documents about the Reconstruction era.

Sharing Scrapbooks

Reader's Reviews

There are numerous ways the class can share what individual students have learned through their scrapbooks. One way is to devote a class period to a quiet reading of the scrapbooks; each student gets to read two to four scrapbooks from start to finish and writes a comment to the author of each one. After I read their comments I pass them along to the scrapbook's creator. When students receive several readers' reviews (See Figure 7.6 and Appendix M), they begin to feel that they have been effective teachers of one another. For the Reconstruction scrapbooks I want the readers to piece together the subject's life based on the documents presented, much as the whole class did with my documents. So I created a form for students to fill in that assesses what they learned from reading a scrapbook. I also want them to convey what they learned about the Reconstruction era as a whole.

Scrapbook Reader's Review

Creator of the Scrapbook: _____ Scrapbook Title _____

Reader of the Scapbook: _____

A.	Facts about the Subject's life.	Documents from which you deduced these facts.
	1.	
	2.	
	3.	
	4.	
	5.	

B.	In the space below, describe one of the most interesting documents included in this scrapbook about life during the Reconstruction era. What did you learn from it and the comments the writer wrote about it:

C.	In the space below summarize what you admire about the subject's life. What were the greatest difficulties he or she faced and his or her greatest accomplishments?

D.	In the space below describe three things you think the creator of this scrapbook did effectively. Describe one thing you think they could have been improved, and tell why.

Fig 7.4 Scrapbook Reader's Review

Monologues, Eulogies, and Obituaries

Another way to share Reconstruction scrapbooks is to ask each student to present a monologue as his or her subject. Alternatively each student can write a eulogy for his or her subject and deliver it to the class. In either case they can present the album as part of the "show and tell." Students can also write an obituary about the person they studied. The Frederick Douglass scrapbooks online at American Memory provide a real-life example; family members collected his obituaries and pasted them into the scrapbooks he kept while alive. (Search the website with keywords such as "Frederick Douglass Death" to find these.) I explain to students that a eulogy is presented orally at a funeral or memorial to a gathering of people who knew the deceased and is meant to praise, whereas an obituary appears in newspapers for the general public and is meant to provide a more objective assessment. In either case, I tell students to describe the person's life within its historical context and to review events we learned about in class.

Holding a Congressional Hearing

An alternative idea for the Reconstruction scrapbook is to hold a Congressional hearing set in 1876 about whether or not federal troops should be withdrawn from the South. African Americans who chose to leave the country or those who resettled in the North can testify about why they left; those remaining in the South can speak about the increasing hardships they will face if the troops leave. Finally, students can write essays addressing the essential questions posed at the start of the unit.

Assessment

The eyewitness scrapbook assignment works well to teach students how to analyze documents and search the Web. This is the intellectual challenge of the assignment, and it is one of a high order. Of all the eyewitness strategies, the scrapbook assignment most engages students in the actual processes by which historians do their work. Because of the excitement it generates, students become fascinated by what documents can tell us. They rise to the challenge of the search itself because it is just plain fun. This in turn helps students overcome their frustrations, especially if the teacher remains highly supportive.

At the same time, the scrapbook assignment holds special appeal to visual learners. The writing it demands—filling in forms and writing captions—is not extensive. Like the other eyewitness strategies, the scrapbook requires students to see history through the eyes of either an imaginary or real person who lived through the time period, and it requires students to learn from one another. Thus, as students learn the methods of historical inquiry, the past becomes palpable and meaningful.

Rubric for Reconstruction Scrapbooks

Topic	Criteria	Mark from 1–5
Cover and Overall Layout	Does your cover include a relevant document? Does it have a strong visual appeal? Have you cut and pasted with neatness and care?	
Time Line	Have you written a time line on the back of every page? Does your time line include dates and information from the textbook and class discussion?	
Document Analysis Worksheet	Have you filled out a Document Analysis Worksheet for every document included? Do the worksheets reflect critical thinking and analysis? Do the worksheets include the URLs in proper bibliographical form for every document?	
Documents About Your Subject	Have you located three documents that reflect something important about your subject's life?	
Documents on Other Aspects of Reconstruction	Have you fulfilled requirements for finding a document on discrimination and intimidation, sharecropping, material culture, and one topic from the optional list?	
Captions	Have you written thoughtful and complete captions for your documents? Do the captions connect the document to the life of your subject in a meaningful way? Do the captions reflect your understanding of this time period in history?	
Overall Comment		

Epilogue

At the beginning of every year I seek out those students who arrive in my class with a love of history; there are always some but never many. These are the students who come forward to tell me in excited voices about the documentary they watched the night before on the History Channel, the historical novel they just finished reading, or the historic site they visited with their parents. I know these students are going to contribute a great deal to our classes because history is already real and meaningful to them. But what about the rest of the class? These are the students I care most about reaching. They begin the year with an understanding that they will learn a lot of facts about the past, but they do not necessarily anticipate that it will be exciting to learn them. The year's challenge lies in teaching these students to love the process of studying history. (In my school we teach social studies up to the eighth grade when students are first exposed to a traditional study of history.)

For these students, the study of dates, facts, and abstract ideas feels unhinged from the reality they know. Not until they can imagine the people who inhabited the past do they care about them and the impact their lives made on our lives today. I have never thought of the study of facts and the uses of the imagination as antithetical to one another. To my mind, the best historians know so much that they can imagine the past with more accuracy and greater empathy than the rest of us. Once I have helped students identify with the past, I can move them to increasingly higher levels of abstract thinking.

My goal in the course of the year is to cover a lot of ground, some of it rapidly and cursorily, but most of it in enough detail that it comes to life. This is where the six eyewitness strategies come in. By interspersing in-depth studies throughout the year, students begin to learn *how* to learn about the past in a meaningful way. Each strategy focuses on a different type of document and connects students to the source by asking them to become authors of similar "documents." Each strategy engages students in a different process and results in a unique project. A year needs variety and new challenges along the way for students, and so too for teachers. The six strategies help me diverisfy what I teach in depth year after year. I already have the strategies in my pocket, and I can pull them out and adapt them to teach different content each year.

It took me many years to develop the potential of each eyewitness strategy, but the discovery and implementation of the very first one—the letter exchange—revolutionized the way I taught. Students learned about the same events from different perspectives, so the controversies they wrote about and argued about in class were no longer dead issues, but living ones.

I would encourage you to experiment with one strategy at a time and to see what happens. If you subsequently implement several over the course of the year, you will notice that bigger things begin to happen. First, the past comes closer in time and students experience the connections among events in a visceral instead of abstract way. For example, one year I staged a Jackson versus Clay election debate followed by a letter exchange set in the turbulent 1850s. Students realized that events of the 1830s were part of the living memory of those whose offspring would fight in the Civil War, and furthermore that there were many cause-and-effect relationships between what happened "then" and "now."

You will find that students get into the swing of participating in history from the eyewitness perspective. For example, my student Dan had some trouble finding the right "voice" at the start of the year when he wrote his Revolutionary War diary. By the time he presented his election speech in favor of Henry Clay, he was living in the past in his imagination and writing about it with ease in the first-person present tense:

The United States of America is still a young country. There are vast parts of our country, such as the west, that are still largely undeveloped and inaccessible. Our national economy will not reach its full strength until all parts of our country are linked together by an efficient transportation system. Until that occurs we will be at a severe competitive disadvantage to Europe. Mr. Henry Clay has a very good plan to reach our economy's full potential. It is called "The American System."

It is Dan's use of verbs that makes this speech so vivid. He uses the present tense to describe what is now to us the past: "The United States is still a young country." Then he switches to future tense: "Our national economy will not reach its full strength until…" That future, which has become our future, hinges upon the decisions people made in the past. Dan's urgent tone expresses that he understands that connection.

One caveat I want to share about the eyewitness strategies is that it can be difficult to incorporate the viewpoints of those who left us no written record—no diaries or travelogues, for example. Indeed, many of these forms of expression are an outgrowth of European society and have no antecedents in other cultures. When Dan describes the West as "undeveloped and inaccessible," he is not speaking for the native peoples living on that land. Insofar as possible, I have tried to show how a multiplicity of voices can be incorporated into the eyewitness strategies, but it is always worth being vigilant. Am I accomplishing what I wish to, and if there are impediments, how can I discuss them and share them with students?

One final thing I learned in writing this book is that far from weakening it, we actually strengthen our students' understanding of democracy by viewing American history from multiple perspectives. The democratic process itself is the best means we have to resolve conflicting opinions and opposing interests. Students need to experience for themselves how and why this is so. All six strategies are based on the premise that in a democracy, people are entitled to freely express their political views both in private and in public. First Amendment rights also include the right to petition the government, a right exercised by women, African Americans, and other groups who were excluded from full citizenship. In looking for ways to share what students have learned at the end of an eyewitness strategy, I want them, if possible, to role-play ways in which conflicts can be resolved using governmental processes such as holding congressional hearings or presidential cabinet meetings.

Through engaging in eyewitness strategies, students also acquire a better understanding of the historian's task: to wade through primary sources that represent competing versions of events, and then to synthesize an interpretation that makes overall sense. This approach to teaching history is not merely fun and engaging (which is wonderful in itself), but it also demands more complex thinking on the part of our students. I know at the end of the year how successful I have been if I can look around and see a classroom full of students who are eager to debate sophisticated ideas and who are excited by the endeavor we have undertaken together.

Appendixes

Appendix A
Chapter 1 Resources: Teaching with Documents

Books and Journals

America Firsthand: Volume One: Readings from Settlement to Reconstruction. 7th ed. Edited by David Burner, Anthony Marcus, and Robert D. Marcus. 2007. New York: Bedford/St. Martin's.

America Firsthand: Volume Two: Readings from Reconstruction to the Present. 7th ed. Edited by David Burner, Anthony Marcus, and Robert D. Marcus. 2007. New York: Bedford/St. Martin's.

At Issue in History. San Diego: Greenhaven. A series with forty-seven titles.

The Boisterous Sea of Liberty: A Documentary History of America from Discovery Through the Civil War. Edited by David Brion Davis and Steven Mintz. 1998. New York: Oxford University Press.

Eyewitness to America: 500 Years of America in the Words of Those Who Saw It Happen. Edited by David Colbert. 1997. New York: Pantheon.

Eyewitness History. 2005. New York: Facts on File. A series with eight titles.

Going to the Source: The Bedford Reader in American History. 2 vols. Edited by Victoria Bissell Brown and Timothy J. Shannon. 2004. New York: Bedford/St. Martin's.

Great Issues in American History. 3 vols. Richard Hofstadter. 1982. New York: Vintage.

Images of America: A Panorama of History in Photographs. Edited by Alexis Doster. 1989. Washington: Smithsonian Books.

Interpreting Primary Documents. San Diego, CA: Greenhaven. A series with twelve titles.

A Larger Memory: A History of Our Diversity with Voices. By Ronald Takaki. 1998. New York: Little Brown.

"The National Archives." Special issue, *Cobblestone Magazine.* 2003. Peterborough, NH: Cobblestone.

Opposing Viewpoints in American History, Volume I: From Colonial Time to Reconstruction. Edited by William Dudley. 2006. Detroit, MI: Greenhaven.

Opposing Viewpoints in American History, Volume II: From Reconstruction to the Present. Edited by William Dudley. 2006. Detroit, MI: Greenhaven.

Our Documents: 100 Milestone Documents from the National Archives. United States National Archives and Records Administration. 2003. New York: Oxford University Press.

Our Documents: A National Initiative on American History, Civics and Service. 3 vols. National History Day. 2002–2004. College Park, MD: National History Day. Available online at http://www.ourdocuments.gov/content.php?page=sourcebook3.

Our Nation's Archive: The History of the United States in Documents. Edited by Erik Bruun and Jay Crosby. 1999. New York: Black Dog and Leventhal.

Photos That Made U.S. History. 2 vols. By Edward Wakin and Daniel Wakin. 1993. New York: Walker.

"Teaching Civics with Primary Documents." Edited by Lee Ann Potter. 2005. *Social Education* 69(7).

"Teaching with Documents Celebrates 25 Years." Edited by Lee Ann Potter. 2002. *Social Education* 66(7).

Teaching with Documents. 13 vols. 2002. Santa Barbara, CA: ABC-CLIO.

Teaching with Documents: Using Primary Sources from the National Archives. 2 vols. Edited by Wynell B. Schamel. 1998. Washington, DC: National Archives and Records Administration.

"Teaching U.S. History with Primary Sources." Edited by Lee Ann Potter. 2003. *Social Education* 67(7).

Witness to America: An Illustrated Documentary History of the United States from the Revolution to Today. Edited by Stephen Ambrose and Douglas Brinkley. 1999. New York: HarperCollins.

Witnessing America. Edited by Noel Rae. 1996. New York: Stonesong.

Websites

"100 Milestone Documents." *Our Documents.gov*. http://www.ourdocuments.gov/content.php?flash=true&page=milestone.
Also includes links to standards.

American Memory. The Library of Congress. http://memory.loc.gov/ammem/index.html.

History Matters: The U.S. Survey Course on the Web. George Mason University. http://historymatters.gmu.edu/.

National Archives and Records Administration. "Educators and Students" section. http://www.archives.gov/education/.

National History Day. http://www.nationalhistoryday.org/.

"Save Our Documents." History Channel. http://www.historychannel. com/classroom/documents/.

Standards

Expectations of Excellence: Curriculum Standards for the Social Studies. 1994. Washington, DC: National Council for the Social Studies. http:// www.socialstudies.org/standards/.

Geography for Life: National Standards for Geography. 1994. Washington: National Geographic Research & Exploration. http://www. nationalgeographic.org/education/standards.html.

Mid-continent Research for Education and Learning (McCrel). 2006 curriculum standards available online. http://www.mcrel.org.

National Standards for Civics and Government. 1997. Calabasas, CA: Center for Civic Education. http://www.civiced.org/stds.html.

National Standards for History: Basic Edition. 1996. Los Angeles: National Center for History in the Schools. http://nchs.ucla.edu/standards/.

Appendix B
Chapter 2 Resources: Diaries

Diaries in American History

Diary of America: The Intimate Story of Our Nation, Told by 100 Diarists—Public Figures and Plain Citizens, Natives and Visitors. By Josef Berger and Dorothy Berger. 1957. New York: Simon and Schuster.

A Diary from Dixie. By Mary Boykin Chestnut. Edited by Ben Ames Williams. 1980. Cambridge, MA: Harvard University Press.

The Diary of Thomas A. Edison. 1970. Old Greenwich, CT: Chatham.

A Free Black Girl Before the Civil War: The Diary of Charlotte Forten, 1854 (Diaries, Letters, and Memoirs). Edited by Christy Steele and Kerry Graves. 1998. Mankato, MN: Capstone.

Growing Up in the 1850s: The Journal of Agnes Lee. Edited by Mary Custis Lee deButts. 1984. Chapel Hill: University of North Carolina Press.

The Haldeman Dairies: Inside the Nixon White House. By H. R. Haldeman. 1994. New York: Putnam.

The Heart of Thoreau's Journals. By Henry David Thoreau. Edited by Odell Shepard. 1961. New York: Dover.

"The Hone Diary." By Philip Hone. In *The Hone and Strong Diaries of Old Manhattan*. Edited by Louis Auchincloss. 1989. New York: Abbeville.

Journal of a Residence on a Georgia Plantation in 1838–1839. By Frances Anne Kemble. Edited by John A. Scott. 1961. New York: Alfred A. Knopf.

The Journals of Louisa May Alcott. Edited by Joel Myerson, Daniel Shealy and Madeleine B. Stern. 1997. Athens: University of Georgia Press.

A Midwife's Tale: The Life of Martha Ballard Based on Her Diary, 1785–1812. By Laurel Thatcher Ulrich. 1990. New York: Alfred A. Knopf.

The Notebooks of F. Scott Fitzgerald. Edited by Matthew J. Bruccoli. 1978. New York: Harcourt, Brace Jovanovich/Bruccoli Clark.

Of Plymouth Plantation: Bradford's History of the Plymouth Settlement 1608–1650. By William Bradford. Edited by Harold Paget. 2006. Mineola, NY: Dover.

The Secret Diary of Harold L. Ickes. 1974. New York: Simon and Schuster.

"The Strong Diary." By George Templeton Strong. In *The Hone and Strong Diaries of Old Manhattan.* Edited by Louis Auchincloss. 1989. New York: Abbeville.

The Wartime Journals of Charles Lindbergh. 1970. New York: Harcourt Brace Jovanovich.

The Colonies and the American Revolution

"An Account of the Slave Trade on the Coast of Africa (1788)." By Alexander Falconbridge. In *Living Documents in American History.* Edited by John Anthony Scott. 1964. New York: Washington Square Books.

American History Told by Contemporaries, Volume II: Building the Republic 1689–1783. By Albert Bushnell Hart. 1924. New York: Macmillan.

The American House: Styles of Architecture. By A. G. Smith. 1983. New York: Dover.

The American Spirit: United States History as Seen by Contemporaries. Thomas A. Bailey. 1963. Boston: D. C. Heath.

April Morning. By Howard Fast. 1961. New York: Bantam Books.

Before the Mayflower: A History of Black America. By Lerone Bennett Jr. 2003. Chicago: Johnson.

"The Boston Massacre: A Paradigm for Developing Thinking and Writing Skills." By Thomas Ladenburg and Geoffrey Tegnell. 1986. *Social Education* 52(1): 71–74.

Colonial Craftsmen and the Beginnings of American Industry. By Edwin Tunis. 1999. Baltimore: John Hopkins University Press.

Colonial Living. By Edwin Tunis. 1999. Baltimore: Johns Hopkins University Press.

Early American Crafts and Occupations Coloring Book. By Peter F. Copeland. 1994. New York: Dover.

Early American Trades Coloring Book. By Peter F. Copeland. 1980. New York: Dover.

Everyday Dress of the American Revolution. By Peter F. Copeland. 1975. New York: Dover.

Great Issues in American History: From Settlement to Revolution 1584–1776. Edited by Richard Hofstadter and Clarence L. Ver Steeg. 1969. New York: Vintage.

Heroes and Heroines of the American Revolution. By Peter F. Copeland. 2004. New York: Dover Pictorial Archives.

"The Interesting Narrative of the Life of Olaudah Equiano or Gustavus Vassa, The African." [1814]. In *The Classic Slave Narratives.* Edited by Henry Louis Gates Jr. 2002. New York: Penguin.

My Brother Sam Is Dead. By James Lincoln Collier and Christopher Collier. 1974. New York: Scholastic.

"'No Taxation Without Representation': A Simulation Activity." By Joan Brodsky Schur. 1992. *Social Education* 56(1): 66–67.

A Reverence for Wood. By Eric Sloane. [1965] 2004. New York: Dover.

The Tavern at the Ferry. By Edwin Tunis. 1973. New York: Ty Crowell.

Websites
Africans in America. PBS. http://www.pbs.org/wgbh/aia/part1/1h281t. html.

"Colonial Williamsburg Trades." Colonial Williamsburg. http://www. history.org/Almanack/life/trades/tradehdr.cfm.
This site provides information on many of colonial trades with accompanying photos and suggestions for further reading.

"A Debate on Natural Rights from Hutchinson's 'A Dialogue Between an American and a European Englishman." *E Pluribus Unum.* Assumption College. http://www.assumption.edu/ahc/1770s/phutchinson.html.
This site includes the letters of Governor Thomas Hutchinson of Massachusetts, whose house was attacked by a mob protesting the Stamp Act.

Famous Trials. University of Missouri-Kansas City. http://www.law. umkc.edu/faculty/projects/ftrials/bostonmassacre/bostonmassacre.html.
This site has a wealth of documentary evidence provided at the trial of the soldiers involved in the Boston Massacre. Paul Revere's propagandistic engraving of the event is a good document with which to begin.

"James Otis, Against the Writs of Assistance, 1761." The Douglass Archives. Northwestern University. http://douglassarchives.org/otis_a34.htm.

Massachusetts Historical Society. http://www.masshist.org/digitaladams/aea/. *Offers portions of John Adams's diary, which can be viewed in its original handwritten form as well as in a modern transcription.*

"A Shoemaker and the Tea Party" and "George Hewes' Recollection of the Boston Massacre." By George Hewes. 1834. In "A Retrospect of the Boston Tea Party." By James Hawkes. History Matters: The U.S. Survey Course on the Web. George Mason University. http://historymatters.gmu.edu/d/5799.

Appendix C
Chapter 3 Resources: Travelogues

Books and Journals

The 1866 Guide to New York City. [1866] 1975. New York: Schocken Books.

An American Exodus: A Record of Human Erosion. By Dorothea Lange and Paul Taylor. [1939] 1999. Paris: Jean-Michel Place.

American Notes for General Circulation. By Charles Dickens. Edited by Patricia Ingham. [1842] 2000. New York: Penguin Classics. Available online through the University of Virginia at http://www.people. virginia.edu/~jlg4p/dickens/titlepg.html.

"An Artist Among the Indians, 1832–39." By George Catlin. In *A Mirror for Americans: Life and Manners in the United States, 1790–1870, as Recorded by American Travelers. Vol. 3. The Frontier Moves West.* Edited by Warren S. Tryon. 1952. Chicago: University of Chicago Press.

Beyond the Divide. By Kathryn Lasky. 1983. New York: Simon and Schuster.

A Briefe and True Report of the New Found Land of Virginia. By Thomas Hariot. [1590] 1972. New York: Dover. Includes 28 engravings. Available online at *Documenting the American South.* University of North Carolina. http://docsouth.unc.edu/nc/hariot/hariot.html.

"Campfire Stories with George Catlin: An Encounter of Two Cultures." Smithsonian Institution. http://catlinclassroom.si.edu/index.html.

Democracy in America. By Alexis de Tocqueville. Edited by Richard D. Heffner. [1835] 2001. New York: Signet Classics. Available online at the University of Virginia. http://xroads.virginia.edu/~Hyper/detoc/.

Domestic Manners of the Americans. By Fanny Trollope. Edited by Pamela Neville-Singington. [1832] 1997. New York: Penguin. Available online at Project Gutenberg. http://www.gutenberg.org/etext/10345.

Journal of a Residence on a Georgian Plantation in 1838–1839. By Frances Anne Kemble. 1984. Athens: University of Georgia Press.

The Journals of Lewis and Clark. By Meriwether Lewis and William Clark. Edited by Bernard DeVoto. 1997. New York: Houghton Mifflin.

The Journals of Lewis and Clark. By Meriwether Lewis and William Clark. 1803–1806. Available online at the University of Virginia. http://xroads.virginia.edu/~Hyper/JOURNALS/toc.html.

Life on the Mississippi. By Mark Twain. [1883] 1983. New York: Bantam. Available online at the Electronic Text Center, University of Virginia Library. http://etext.virginia.edu/toc/modeng/public/TwaLife.html.

Migrant Farm Families. By Dorothea Lange. A collection of photographs at the History Place. Philip Gavin. http://www.historyplace.com/index.html.

A Mirror for Americans: Life and Manners in the United States 1790–1870 as Recorded by American Travelers, Volume 3: The Frontier Moves West. By Warren S. Tryon. 1952. Chicago: University of Chicago Press.

On the Road. By Jack Kerouac. [1959] 1991. New York: Penguin.

The Oregon Trail. By Francis Parkman. [1849] 2002. Mineola, NY: Dover. Available online at the University of Virginia. http://xroads.virginia.edu/~Hyper/OREGON/oregon.html.

Pioneer Women: Voices from the Kansas Frontier. By Joanna L. Stratton. 1981. New York: Simon and Schuster.

Retrospect of Western Travel. By Harriet Martineau. Edited by Daniel Feller. [1838] 2000. Armonk, NY: M.E. Sharpe.

Roughing It. By Mark Twain. [1872] 1994. New York: Signet Classics. Available online at Electronic Text Center, University of Virginia Library. http://etext.virginia.edu/toc/modeng/public/TwaRoug.html.

The Slave States, Before the Civil War. By Frederick Law Olmstead. Edited by Harvey Wish. [1856] 1959. New York: Capricorn.

Society in America. By Harriet Martineau. Edited by Seymore Martin Lipset. [1837] 1981. Somerset, NJ: Transaction. Available online at the Dead Sociologists Society. http://www2.pfeiffer.edu/~lridener/DSS/Martineau/siatoc.html.

A Tour of the Prairies. By Washington Irving. 1835. Edited by John F. McDermott. 1985. Norman: University of Oklahoma Press. Available online at Electronic Text Center, University of Virginia Library. http://etext.virginia.edu/toc/modeng/public/IrvTour.html.

Travels with Charley: In Search of America. By John Steinbeck. [1962] 2002. New York: Penguin.

A Treasury of Railroad Folklore. Edited by B. A. Botkin and Alvin F. Harlow. 1954. New York: Bonanza.

Two Years Before the Mast: A Personal Narrative of Life at Sea. By Richard Henry Dana Jr. [1841] 2000. New York: Signet Classics. Available online at Electronic Text Center, University of Virginia Library. http://etext.lib.virginia.edu/toc/modeng/public/DanTwoy.html.

The West: Contemporary Records of America's Expansion Across the Continent: 1607–1890. Edited by Bayrd Still. 1975. New York: Capricorn.

The WPA Guide to New Orleans: The Federal Writers' Project Guide to 1930s New Orleans. [1938] 1983. New York: Pantheon.

The WPA Guide to New York City: The Federal Writers' Project Guide to 1930s New York. [1939] 1982. New York: Pantheon.

Websites

"American Indians of the Pacific Northwest." American Memory, Library of Congress. http://memory.loc.gov/ammem/award98/wauhtml/aipnhome.html.

"American Journeys: Eyewitness Accounts of Early American Exploration and Settlement." Wisconsin Historical Society. http://www.americanjourneys.org/.

"American Notes: Travels in America, 1750–1920." American Memory, Library of Congress. http://lcweb2.loc.gov/ammem/lhtnhtml/lhtnhome.html.

"California As I Saw It: First Person Narratives of California's Early Years, 1849–1900." American Memory, Library of Congress. http://memory.loc.gov/ammem/cbhtml/cbhome.html.

"Discovery and Exploration." American Memory, Library of Congress. http://rs6.loc.gov/ammem/gmdhtml/dsxphome.html.

"Dustbowl Days." EDSITEment, National Endowment for the Humanities. http://edsitement.neh.gov/view_lesson_plan.asp?id=300.

"The First American West: The Ohio River Valley 1750–1820." American Memory, Library of Congress. http://memory.loc.gov/ammem/award99/icuhtml/fawhome.html.

"Heading West: Mapping the Territory" and "Touring West: 19th-century Performing Artists on the Overland Trails." New York Public Library. http://www.nypl.org/west/index.html.

"The Hudson River School." In *Timeline of Art History*. The Metropolitan Museum of Art. http://www.metmuseum.org/toah/hd/hurs/hd_hurs.htm.

"Map Collections." American Memory, Library of Congress. http://memory.loc.gov/ammem/gmdhtml/gmdhome.html.

"New Perspectives on the West." PBS. http://www.pbs.org/weta/thewest/.

"The Oregon Trail." By Steve Boettcher and Mike Trinklein. http://www.isu.edu/%7Etrinmich/Oregontrail.html.

"Panoramic Maps 1847–1929." American Memory, Library of Congress. http://memory.loc.gov/ammem/pmhtml/panhome.html.

"Photographs of the American West: 1861-1912." U.S. National Archives and Records Administration. http://www.archives.gov/research/american-west/.

Appendix D
Chapter 4 Resources: Letters

Books and Journals
American Letters series. Edited by Joan Brodsky Schur. Interact. 1986. Fort Atkinson, WI: Interact.

The Book of Abigail and John: Selected Letters of the Adams Family 1762–1784. By John Adams and Abigail Adams. Edited by L. H. Butterfield, Marc Friedlaender, and Mary-Jo Kline. 1975. Cambridge, MA: Harvard University Press.

The Children of Pride: A True Story of Georgia and the Civil War. Edited by Robert Manson Myers. 1984. New Haven, CT: Yale University Press.

Dear Mrs. Roosevelt: Letters from Children of the Great Depression. Edited by Robert Cohen. 2002. Chapel Hill: University of North Carolina Press.

Eleanor and Harry: The Correspondence of Eleanor Roosevelt and Harry S. Truman. Edited by Steve Neal. 2002. New York: Kensington.

The First Forty Years of Washington Society. Margaret Bayard Smith. 1906. New York: Charles Scribner's Sons.

"Learning About the Civil War Through Soldiers' Letters." By Joseph Hutchinson. 2005. *Social Education* 69(6): 318–322.

"Letter Exchanges: Living Through the Past in a Fictional Correspondence." By Joan Brodsky Schur. 1984. *Social Education* 48(4): 278–279.

Letters in American History: Words to Remember. Edited by Jack H. Lang. 1982. New York: Harmony.

The Timetables of American History. Edited by Lawrence Urdang. 2001. New York: Touchstone.

Women's Letters: America from the Revolutionary War to the Present. Edited by Lisa Grunwald and Stephen Adler. 2005. New York: Dial.

Websites

"America's First Look into the Camera: 1839–1862." American Memory, Library of Congress. http://memory.loc.gov/ammem/daghtml/ daghome.html.

"Battle Lines: Letters from America's Wars." Gilder Lehrman Institute of American History. http://www.gilderlehrman.org/collection/battlelines/ index_good.html.

"Civil War Letters." By Joan Brodsky Schur. PBS. http://www.pbs. org/civilwar/classroom/lesson_letters.html.

"Correspondence Between John Adams and Abigail Adams." Massachusetts Historical Society. http://www.masshist.org/DIGITALADAMS/ AEA/letter/.

Correspondence on the Rosenbergs Between Clyde R. Miller and Dwight D. Eisenhower. 1953. Available online at http://www.eisenhower. archives.gov/dl/Rosenbergs/11.pdf and http://www.eisenhower.archives. gov/dl/Rosenbergs/Binder12.pdf.

"The Digital Documents Project." Dwight D. Eisenhower Presidential Library and Museum. http://www.eisenhower.archives.gov/dl/hd.htm.

"Letters and Diaries." By Edward L. Ayers. *Valley of the Shadow: Two Communities in the American Civil War.* Virginia Center for Digital History. http://valley.vcdh.virginia.edu/.

Appendix E
Chapter 5 Resources: Newspapers

Books and Journals

A Bintel Brief: Sixty Years of Letters from the Lower East Side to the Jewish Daily Forward. Edited by Isaac Metzker. 1971. New York: Schocken.

Extraordinary Women Journalists. By Claire Price-Groff. 1998. Chicago: Children's Press.

The Greenwood Library of American War Reporting. 8 vols. Edited by David A. Copeland. 2004. Westport, CT: Greenwood.

Hospital Sketches: An Army Nurse's True Account of Her Experience During the Civil War. By Louisa May Alcott. [1869] 1986. Boston: Applewood.

Reporting Civil Rights. 2 vols. Edited by Clayborne Carson. 2003. New York: Library of America.

Reporting World War Two. 2 vols. Edited by Anne Matthews, Nancy Caldwell Sorel, and Roger J. Spiller. 1995. New York: Library of America.

"Students as Newspaper Reporters During the Civil War." By Joan Brodsky Schur. 1989. *Social Education* January: 69–71.

Tell Me No Lies: Investigative Journalism That Changed the World. Edited by John Pilger. 2005. New York: Thunder's Mouth.

The Vintage Mencken. By H. L. Mencken. Edited by Alistair Cooke. 1990. New York: Vintage.

Walt Whitman's Civil War. By Walt Whitman. Edited by Walter Lowenfels. 1960. New York: Da Capo.

Websites

Article Archive 1851–Present. *New York Times.* http://www.nytimes.com/.

"Be the Press: Local Interviews, National News." By Syd Golston and Lisa Greeves. NewsHour Extra, PBS. http://www.pbs.org/newshour/extra/teachers/lessonplans/socialstudies/Vote2004/newswriting.html.

"The Black Press: Soldiers Without Swords." PBS. http://www.pbs.org/blackpress/.

"The Brooklyn Daily Eagle 1841–1902." Brooklyn Public Library. http://www.brooklynpubliclibrary.org/eagle/.

Center for Media Literacy. http://www.medialit.org.

"Chicago Defender Historical Archive." Chicago Public Library. http://www.chipublib.org/003cpl/hf/hf06/cdha.html.

"Choices for the 21st Century." The Choices Program, Watson Institute for International Studies at Brown University. http://www.choices.edu/.

"Civil War-Era Newspapers." By Edward L. Ayers. Valley of the Shadow: Two Communities in the American Civil War. Virginia Center for Digital History. http://valley.vcdh.virginia.edu/.

"Civil War Newspapers." By Vicki Betts. University of Texas at Tyler. http://www.uttyler.edu/vbetts/newspaper_titles.htm.

"Conflicting Newspaper Accounts." By Joan Brodsky Schur. PBS. http://www.pbs.org/civilwar/classroom/lesson_letters.html.

"*Harpers Weekly Journal of Civilization*, 1857–1912." *Harper's Weekly.* http://www.harpweek.com/04Products/products-Explained.asp.

"Learning Network." *New York Times* on the Web. http://www.nytimes.com/learning/.

"Making Sense of Advertisements." By Daniel Pope. History Matters: The U.S. Survey Course on the Web. http://historymatters.gmu.edu/mse/Ads/.

"Reporting America at War." PBS. http://www.pbs.org/weta/reportingamericaatwar/.

"Wilson and African Americans." By Joan Brodsky Schur. PBS. http://www.pbs.org/wgbh/amex/wilson/tguide/t_lesson_02.html.

"Women Come to the Front: Journalists, Photographers, and Broadcasters During World War Two." The Library of Congress. http://www.loc.gov/exhibits/wcf/.

Appendix F
Chapter 6 Resources: Election Speeches

Books and Journals

Abe Lincoln in Illinois. By Robert E. Sherwood. 1937. New York: Dramatists Play Service.

The American Heritage Book of Great American Speeches for Young People. Edited by Suzanne McIntire. 2001. New York: John Wiley and Sons.

American History Re-creations series. Interact. Fort Atkinson, WI: Highsmith. http://www.highsmith.com.

The American Presidency. By Clinton Rossiter. [1960] 1987. Baltimore, MD: Johns Hopkins University Press.

American Voices: Significant Speeches in American History, 1640–1945. Edited by James Andrews and David Zarefsky. 1989. New York: Longman.

Basic Debate: 4th Edition. By Leslie Phillips, William S. Hicks, Douglas R. Springer, and Maridell Fryar. 2001. Chicago: Glencoe McGraw-Hill.

Contemporary American Voices: Significant Speeches in American History, 1945–Present. Edited by James Andrews and David Zarefsky. 1991. New York: Longman.

Great Speeches in History: Women's Rights. Edited by Jennifer A. Hurley. 2002. San Diego, CA: Greenhaven.

"A Guide to the Presidential Debates." 2004. *Social Education* 68(5): 325–330.

"History Comes Alive—A Hypothetical Election Debate." By Joan Brodsky Schur. 1978. *The Social Studies* 69(4): 177–179.

In Our Own Words: Extraordinary Speeches of the American Century. Edited by Robert Torricelli and Andrew Carroll. 1999. New York: Simon and Schuster.

Lincoln at Gettysburg: The Words That Remade America. By Gary Wills. 1992. New York: Simon and Schuster.

My Fellow Americans: The Most Important Speeches of America's Presidents, from George Washington to George W. Bush. Edited by Michael Waldman. 2003. Naperville, IL: Sourcebooks.

Oratorical Culture in Nineteenth-Century America: Transformations in the Theory and Practice of Rhetoric. Edited by Gregory Clark and S. Michael Halloran. 1993. Carbondale, IL: Southern Illinois University Press.

Pioneer Women Orators: Rhetoric in the Ante-Bellum Reform Movement. Lillian O'Connor. 1954. New York: Columbia University Press.

"Teaching the Election Process in Ten Days." By S. Kay Gandy. 2004. *Social Education* 68: 332–340.

Websites

"American Experience: The Presidents." WGBH and PBS. http://www.pbs.org/wgbh/amex/presidents/index.html.

"The AmericanPresident.org." University of Virginia. http://www.americanpresident.org/.

"American Rhetoric: Online Speech Bank." By Michael E. Eidenmuller. http://www.americanrhetoric.com/speechbank.htm.

"America Votes: Presidential Campaign Memorabilia from the Duke University Special Collections Library." Duke University. http://scriptorium.lib.duke.edu/americavotes/.

"Analyze Abolitionist Speeches." History Matters: The U.S. Survey Course on the Web. http://historymatters.gmu.edu/mse/sia/speeches.htm.

"Angelina Weld Grimké Speech at Pennsylvania Hall." WGBH and PBS. http://www.pbs.org/wgbh/aia/home.html.

"Born to Command: King Andrew the First." (Cartoon.) National Archives and Records Administration. http://www.archives.gov/exhibits/treasures_of_congress/Images/page_9/30a.html.

"Debate Transcripts." Commission on Presidential Debates. http://www.debates.org/.

"Herblock's History: Political Cartoons from the Crash to the Millennium." Library of Congress. http://www.loc.gov/rr/print/swann/herblock/.

"It's No Laughing Matter: Analyzing Political Cartoons." American Memory, Library of Congress. http://memory.loc.gov/ammem/.

League of Women Voters. http://www.lwv.org//AM/Template.cfm?Section=Home.

"Old Jack, the famous New Orleans mouser, clearing Uncle Sam's Barn of Bank and Clay Rats." (Cartoon.) *Harper's Weekly*. http://loc.harpweek.com/LCPoliticalCartoons/DisplayCartoonMedium.asp?MaxID=&UniqueID=9&Year=1832&YearMark=.

"Political Memorabilia." The Ohio Historical Society. http://www.cyberbee.com/campaign/mem.html.

"Political Speeches." By Allan Louden. Wake Forest University. http://www.wfu.edu/~louden/Political%20Communication/Class%20Information/SPEECHES.html.
Includes links to audio data banks.

"The Presidents of the United States." By White House Historical Association. The White House. http://www.whitehouse.gov/history/presidents/index.html.

Project Vote Smart. http://www.vote-smart.org/index.htm.

"The Seventh of March Speech." By Daniel Webster. 1850. Dartmouth College. http://www.dartmouth.edu/~dwebster/speeches/seventh-march.html.

"What to the Slave Is the Fourth of July?" By Frederick Douglass. Douglass Archives of American Public Address. http://douglassarchives.org/doug_a10.htm.

Appendix G
Chapter 7 Resources: Scrapbooks

Scrapbooks, Lessons, and Primary Sources

"Analysis of Primary Sources." American Memory, Library of Congress. http://memory.loc.gov/learn/lessons/psources/analyze.html.

"Black History Remains Alive in Alexander Gumby's Popular Scrapbooks." By Jo Kadlecek. Columbia University. http://www.columbia.edu/cu/news/02/02/alexanderGumby.html.

"Document Analysis Worksheets." U. S. National Archives and Records Administration. http://www.archives.gov/education/lessons/worksheets/.

"Doing the Decades: Group Investigations in Twentieth Century U.S. History." By William R. Fernekes and Harlene Rosenberg. American Memory, Library of Congress. http://memory.loc.gov/learn/lessons/97/week/whome.html.

"Every Picture Has a Story." Smithsonian Education. http://www.smithsonianeducation.org/educators/lesson_plans/every_picture/index.html.

"Figuring Somepin 'Bout the Great Depression." By Amy McElroy and Chris Pietsch. American Memory, Library of Congress. http://rs6.loc.gov/ammem/ndlpedu/lessons/99/migrant/intro.html.

"The Lewis Carroll Scrapbook Collection." Rare Book and Special Collections Division, Library of Congress. http://international.loc.gov/intldl/carrollhtml/lchome.html.

"Mark Twain." PBS. http://www.pbs.org/marktwain/.

"Miller NAWSA Suffrage Scrapbooks, 1897–1911." American Memory, Library of Congress. http://memory.loc.gov/ammem/collections/

suffrage/millerscrapbooks/.

"Ohio Memory: an Online Scrapbook of Ohio History." Ohio Memory, Ohio Historical Society. http://www.ohiomemory.org.

"Search for Family History Scrapbooks." The Statue of Liberty-Ellis Island Foundation. http://webcenter.ellisisland.netscape.com/scrapbooks/wscbs_2.asp.

"Self Works: Diaries, Scrapbooks, and Other Autobiographical Efforts." University of Delaware Library, Special Collections Department. http://www.lib.udel.edu/ud/spec/exhibits/selfwork/.

"Scrapbooks." By Susan Tucker. Tulane University. http://www.tulane.edu/~wclib/scrapbooks.html.

Scrapbooking Supplies Online. http://www.scrapbookingsuppliesonline.com/index.asp.

African American History

"Africans in America." PBS. http://www.pbs.org/wgbh/aia/home.html.

"African American History." American Memory, Library of Congress. http://memory.loc.gov/ammem/browse/ListSome.php?category=African%20American%20History.

"African American Lives: Analyzing the Evidence." PBS. http://www.pbs.org/wnet/aalives/analyzing.html.

"Biographies." By Tanya Bolden. Digital Schomburg African American Women Writers of the 19th Century, New York Public Library. http://digital.nypl.org/schomburg/writers_aa19/biographies.html.

Black Saga: The African American Experience: A Chronology. By Charles M. Christian. 1999. Washington, D.C.: Civitas Counterpoint.

"The Bureau of Refugees, Freedmen, and Abandoned Lands." By Kahlil Chism. 2006. *Social Education* 70 (1): 19–26.

"The Emancipation Proclamation." U. S. National Archives and Records Administration. http://www.archives.gov/exhibits/featured_documents/emancipation_proclamation/

"The Frederick Douglass Papers at the Library of Congress." American Memory, Library of Congress. http://memory.loc.gov/ammem/doughtml/doughome.html.

"Images of 19th Century African Americans." Digital Schomburg, New York Public Library. http://digital.nypl.org/cgi-shl/vsc30b.exe/schomburg/images_aa19/toc.html?E+nyplbeta.

"Reconstruction: The Second Civil War." PBS. http://www.pbs.org/wgbh/amex/reconstruction/.

"The Rise and Fall of Jim Crow." PBS. http://www.pbs.org/wnet/jimcrow/.

"Sealing the Sacred Bonds of Holy Matrimony: Freedmen's Bureau Marriage Records." By Reginald Washington. 2005. Prologue 37. http://www.archives.gov/publications/prologue/2005/spring/freedman-marriage-recs.html.

"Teaching With Documents: The Fight for Equal Rights: Black Soldiers in the Civil War." By Budge Weidman. U. S. National Archives and Records Administration. http://www.archives.gov/education/lessons/blacks-civil-war/article.html.

"This Far by Faith: African-American Spiritual Journeys." PBS. http://www.pbs.org/thisfarbyfaith/.

"Time Line of African American History, 1852–1880." American Memory, Library of Congress. http://memory.loc.gov/ammem/aap/timeline.html.

Appendix H

Photo Analysis Worksheet

Step 1. Observation

| A. | Study the photograph for 2 minutes. Form an overall impression of the photograph and then examine individual items. Next, divide the photo into quadrants and study each section to see what new details become visible. |

| B. | Use the chart below to list people, objects, and activities in the photograph. |

People	Objects	Activities

Step 2. Inference

Based on what you have observed above, list three things you might infer from this photograph.

Step 3. Questions

| A. | What questions does this photograph raise in your mind? |

| B. | Where could you find answers to them? |

Designed and developed by the
Education Staff, National Archives and Records Administration, Washington, DC 20408.

Page URL: http://www.archives.gov/education/lessons/worksheets/photo.html

The U.S. National Archives and Records Administration
8601 Adelphi Road, College Park, MD 20740-6001 • Telephone: 1-86-NARA-NARA or 1-866-272-6272

Appendix I

Advertisement Analysis Worksheet

A.		In what publication did this advertisement appear? What is the date of publication?
B.		Who created the advertisement?
C.		What is the purpose of the advertisement?
D.		Who is the intended audience for the advertisement?
E.		If a product is being sold, what strategies does the ad use to convince the target audience that they should want this product?
F.		How common or unique was this product for its era?
G.		What does the advertisement tell us about material life in America at this time?
H.		What does the advertisement tell us about social relationships in America at this time?

Appendix J

Cartoon Analysis Worksheet

Level 1	
Visuals	Words (not all cartoons include words)
1. List the objects or people you see in the cartoon.	1. Identify the cartoon caption and/or title. 2. Locate three words or phrases used by the cartoonist to identify objects or people within the cartoon. 3. Record any important dates or numbers that appear in the cartoon.

Level 2	
Visuals	Words
2. Which of the objects on your list are symbols? 3. What do you think each symbol means?	4. Which words or phrases in the cartoon appear to be the most significant? Why do you think so? 5. List adjectives that describe the emotions portrayed in the cartoon.

Level 3

A. Describe the action taking place in the cartoon.

B. Explain how the words in the cartoon clarify the symbols.

C. Explain the message of the cartoon.

D. What special interest groups would agree/disagree with the cartoon's message? Why?

Page URL: http://www.archives.gov/education/lessons/worksheets/cartoon.html

The U.S. National Archives and Records Administration
8601 Adelphi Road, College Park, MD 20740-6001 • Telephone: 1-86-NARA-NARA or 1-866-272-6272

Appendix K

Document Analysis Worksheet

Your Name _____   Title of Document _____

A.	Is your document (check one) ☐ Issued by a governmental agency? ☐ Issued by a private organization? ☐ A contract between two private citizens? How do you know? Explain:_____ _____ _____
B.	When was it issued? _____ To whom was it issued? _____ By whom was it issued? _____
C.	Are there any seals on the document, and what do they tell us? _____ _____
D.	Are there any signatures on the document, and if so what do they tell us? _____ _____
E.	To what does the certificate or legal document attest or certify? _____ _____
F.	Why might it be important for the agency or person who issued this document to retain such a record? _____ _____
G.	Why might it be important for the recipient to keep a copy? _____ _____
H.	What can we learn about the recipient's life from this document? _____ _____
I.	What can we learn about this time period in history from this document? _____ _____

Adapted from worksheets from the National Archives Digital Classroom and the Learning Page of the Library of Congress.

Appendix L

Debate Score Sheet

Topic: [The Bank War] _____

TEAM: [Andrew Jackson] _____ DEBATOR [Marcus Adams] _____

ARGUMENTS:	Did the speaker present convincing, well-reasoned ideas supported by facts?
REBUTTAL:	Did the speaker give a point for point refutation of the opponent's speech, presenting well-reasoned arguments and facts?
PRESENTATION:	Were the constructive and rebuttal speeches delivered in a clear, forceful, and convincing manner? Did the speaker win your trust?
SCORE:	1-5 points with 5 the highest score possible. __ Constructive Arguments __ Rebuttal __ Presentation

Promotional Materials Score Card

TEAM: _____ NAME OF STUDENT _____

A.	Check item produced: ☐ Poster ☐ Flyer ☐ Buttons ☐ Bumper Stickers ☐ Radio or TV Ads ☐ Political Cartoon ☐ Other _____
B.	Score: 1-5 point with 5 the highest score possible. ____ 1. Was the message of the promotional material clear? ____ 2. Did it reflect an understanding of the issues in the campaign? ____ 3. Was it produced with creativity and care? ____ 4. Was it clever and did it carry emotional punch?

Appendix M

Scrapbook Reader's Review

Creator of the Scrapbook: _____   Scrapbook Title _____

Reader of the Scapbook: _____

A.		Facts about the Subject's life.	Documents from which you deduced these facts.
		1.	
		2.	
		3.	
		4.	
		5.	

B.   In the space below, describe one of the most interesting documents included in this scrapbook about life during the Reconstruction era. What did you learn from it and the comments the writer wrote about it:
_____
_____
_____
_____

C.   In the space below summarize what you admire about the subject's life. What were the greatest difficulties he or she faced and his or her greatest accomplishments?
_____
_____
_____
_____

D.   In the space below describe three things you think the creator of this scrapbook did effectively. Describe one thing you think they could have been improved, and tell why.
_____
_____
_____
_____

References

Adams, John. "Reflections on the Boston Massacre." Massachusetts Historical Society. http://www.masshist.org/adams/.

American Memory. "The Frederick Douglass Papers at the Library of Congress." American Memory, Library of Congress. http://memory.loc.gov/ammem/doughtml/doughome.html.

Appleby, Joyce, Alan Brinkley, and James M. McPherson. 2003. *The American Journey*. New York: Glencoe McGraw-Hill.

Ayers, Edward L. 2003–2006. "The Freedman's Spelling-Book." Valley of the Shadow: Two Communities in the American Civil War. http://valley.vcdh.virginia.edu/HIUS403/freedmen/bigbook.html.

Barton, Keith C., and Linda Levstik. 2004. *Teaching History for the Common Good*. Mahwah, N J: Lawrence Erlbaum.

Bias, Danielle, Rebecca Black, and Susan Tucker. "Scrapbooks and Albums, Theories and Practice: An Annotated Bibliography." Tulane University. http://www.tulane.edu/~wclib/susan.html.

Botkin, B. A., and Alvin F. Harlow, eds. 1953. *A Treasury of Railroad Folklore*. New York: Bonanza.

Brands, H. W. 2005. *Andrew Jackson: His Life and Times*. New York: Random House.

Byrd, William. 1941. *The Secret Diary of William Byrd of Westover, 1709–1712*, ed. Louis B. Wright and Marion Tinling. Richmond: Dietz.

Carr, Caleb. 2003. "William Pitt the Elder and the Avoidance of the American Revolution." In *What Ifs? of American History: Eminent Historians Imagine What Might Have Been*, ed. Robert Cowley. New York: Berkley.

Catlin, George. [1841] 1952. "An Artist Among the Indians, 1832–39." In *A Mirror for Americans: Life and Manners in the United States 1790–1870 as Recorded by American Travelers, Vol. 3, The Frontier Moves West*, ed. Warren S. Tryon. Chicago: University of Chicago Press.

Charleston Mercury. 1864. "The Exiles from Atlanta." *Charleston Mercury*. September 27:p. 1, c. 2. Available online at Civil War Newspapers, a site maintained by Vicki Betts, University of Texas at Tyler. http://www.uttyler.edu/vbetts/charleston_mercury_pt2.htm.

Clark, Gregory, and S. Michael Halloran, eds. 1993. *Oratorical Culture in Nineteenth-Century America: Transformations in the Theory and Practice of Rhetoric*. Carbondale: Southern Illinois University Press.

Collier, James Lincoln, and Christopher Collier. 1974. *My Brother Sam Is Dead*. New York: Scholastic.

Cowley, Robert, ed. 2003. *What Ifs? of American History: Eminent Historians Imagine What Might Have Been*. New York: Berkley.

Dickens, Charles. [1842] 1972. *American Notes for General Circulation: Revised Edition*. New York: Penguin.

Douglass, Frederick. [1845] 2003. *Narrative of the Life of Frederick Douglass*. New York: Barnes and Noble.

———. 1852. "What to the Slave Is the Fourth of July?" Douglass Archives of American Public Address. http://douglassarchives.org/.

Dudley, William. 1996. *Opposing Viewpoints in American History, Volumes 1 and 2*. San Diego, CA: Greenhaven.

Duffey, E. B. 1877. *The Ladies and Gentlemen's Etiquette: A Complete Manual of the Manners and Dress of American Society Containing Forms of Letters, Invitations, Acceptances and Regrets With a Copious Index*. Philadelphia: Porter and Coates.

Earle, Alice Morse. [1898] 1993. *Home Life in Colonial Days.* Stockbridge, MA: Berkshire House.

Eaton, Jana Sackman. 2004. "Using Comparative Online Media to Study the Iraq War." *Social Education* 68(3): 190–194.

Fast, Howard. 1961. *April Morning.* New York: Bantam Books.

Fernekes, William R., and Harlene Rosenberg. "Doing the Decades: Group Investigations in Twentieth-Century U.S. History." American Memory, Library of Congress. http://memory.loc.gov/learn/lessons/97/week/whome.html.

Garraty, John A. 1991. *The Story of America.* Chicago: Holt, Rinehart, and Winston.

Goldman, Arnold, and John S. Whitley, eds. 1972. "Introduction." In Charles Dickens' *American Notes for General Circulation: Revised Edition.* New York: Penguin.

Golston, Syd, and Lisa Greeves. "Be the Press: Local Interviews, National News." PBS Online. http://www.pbs.org/newshour/extra/teachers/lessonplans/socialstudies/Vote2004/newswriting.html.

Grimké Weld, Angelina. 1838. "Angelina Grimké Weld's Speech at Pennsylvania Hall." http://www.pbs.org/wgbh/aia/part4/4h2939t.html.

Harper's Weekly Journal of Civilization. 1865a. "The Southern People Undeceived." *Harper's Weekly Journal of Civilization*, March 18.

Harper's Weekly Journal of Civilization. 1865b. "A Visit to Fort Sumter." *Harper's Weekly Journal of Civilization*, March 18.

HarpWeek. "Freedman's Bureau! An Agency to Keep the Negro in Idleness at the Expense of the White Man." American Political Prints,

1766–1876. HarpWeek. http://loc.harpweek.com/LCPoliticalCartoons/DisplayCartoonMedium.asp?MaxID=&UniqueID=6&Year=1866&YearMark=.

———. "Old Jack, the famous New Orleans mouser, clearing Uncle Sam's Barn of Bank and Clay Rats." HarpWeek. http://loc.harpweek.com/LCPoliticalCartoons/DisplayCartoonMedium.asp?MaxID=&UniqueID=9&Year=1832&YearMark=.

Hofstadtler, Richard. 1958. *Great Issues in American History: From the Revolution to the Civil War.* New York: Vintage.

Ladenburg, Thomas, and Geoffrey Tegnell. 1986. "The Boston Massacre: A Paradigm for Developing Thinking and Writing Skills." *Social Education* 40(1): 71–74.

Lawrence, Jerome, and Robert E. Lee. [1955] 2003. *Inherit the Wind.* New York: Ballantine.

Lorcin, Patricia M. E. "Women's Travel Writing." Center for History and New Media. George Mason University. http://chnm.gmu.edu/worldhistorysources/d/146/whm.html.

Lowenfels, Walter, ed. 1961. *Walt Whitman's Civil War.* New York: Alfred A. Knopf.

Mallon, Thomas. 1984. *A Book of One's Own: People and Their Diaries.* St. Paul: Hungry Mind.

McCrel (Mid-continent Research for Education and Learning). 2006. http://www.mcrel.org/#.

Melvin, L. Rebecca Johnson, curator. 2003. "Self Works: Diaries, Scrapbooks, and Other Autobiographical Efforts." University of Delaware. http://www.lib.udel.edu/ud/spec/exhibits/selfwork/.

Miller, Elizabeth Smith, and Anne Fitzhugh Miller. "Miller NAWSA Suffrage Scrapbooks, 1897–1911." American Memory, Library of Congress. http://memory.loc.gov/ammem/collections/suffrage/millerscrapbooks/.

Myers, Robert Manson, ed. 1984. *The Children of Pride: A True Story of Georgia and the Civil War*. New Haven: Yale University Press.

National Center for History in the Schools. *National Standards for History: Basic Edition*. 1996. Los Angeles: National Center for History in the Schools.

National Council for the Social Studies. 1994. *Expectations of Excellence: Curriculum Standards for the Social Studies*. Washington, D.C.: National Council for the Social Studies.

O'Connor, Lillian. 1954. *Pioneer Women Orators: Rhetoric in the Ante-Bellum Reform Movement*. New York: Columbia University Press.

Olsen, Ken. 2006. "Discovering Lewis & Clark" in *Teaching Tolerance* 29: 38–43.

PBS Online. "Mark Twain's Interactive Scrapbook." PBS Online. http://www.pbs.org/marktwain/scrapbook/index.html.

Pope, Daniel. "Making Sense of Advertisements." History Matters: The U.S. Survey Course on the Web. http://historymatters.gmu.edu/mse/Ads/.

Post, Emily. 1922. *Etiquette in Society, in Business, in Politics and at Home*. Bartleby.com. http://www.bartleby.com/95/.

Rossiter, Clinton. [1956] 1987. *The American Presidency*. New York: Johns Hopkins University Press.

Schur, Joan Brodsky. 1986. American Letters series. Fort Atkinson, WI: Interact/Highsmith.

———. 1992. " 'No Taxation Without Representation': A Simulation Activity." *Social Education* 56:66–67.

———. 2001. "Wilson and African Americans." PBS Online. http://www.pbs.org/wgbh/amex/wilson/tguide/t_lesson_02.html.

Sewall, Samuel. 1968. "From the Diary." In *American Literature Survey: Colonial and Federal to 1800*, ed. Seymour L. Gross and Milton R. Stern. New York: Viking.

Sheriff, Carol. "Preserving the Sabbath." New York State Erie Canal Archives Time Machine. http://www.archives.nysed.gov/projects/eriecanal/ErieEssay/sab.html.

Sherwood, Robert E. 1937. *Abe Lincoln in Illinois.* New York: Dramatists Play Service.

Smith, Margaret Bayard. "A Letter to Mrs. Kirkpatrick, March 11, 1829." Description of Jackson's Inaugural available at the White House Historical Association. http://www.whitehousehistory.org/04/subs/1828_b.html.

———. 1906. *The First Forty Years of Washington Society*. New York: Charles Scribner's Sons.

Stampp, Kenneth. 1965. *The Era of Reconstruction, 1865–1877*. New York: Vintage.

Stille, Alexander. 2002. "Textbook Publishers Learn to Avoid Messing with Texas." *New York Times,* June 29.

Stowe, Steven. 2002. "Making Sense of Letters and Diaries." History Matters: The U.S. Survey Course on the Web. http://www.historymatters.gmu.edu/mse/letters/.

Trollope, Fanny. [1832] 1927. *Domestic Manners of the Americans.* London: George Rutledge.

Tryon, Warren S. 1952. *A Mirror for Americans: Life and Manners in the United States 1790–1870 as Recorded by American Travelers, Vol. 3, The Frontier Moves West.* Chicago: University of Chicago Press.

Tucker, Susan. "Scrapbooks." Tulane University. http://www.tulane.edu/~wclib/scrapbooks.html.

Twain, Mark. [1872] 1994. *Roughing It.* New York: Signet Classics.

———. [1883] 1983. *Life on the Mississippi.* New York: Bantam.

Urdang, Laurence. 2001. *The Timetables of American History.* New York: Touchstone.

U.S. National Archives and Records Administration. "Born to Command: King Andrew the First." U.S. National Archives and Records Administration. http://www.archives.gov/exhibits/treasures_of_congress/Images/page_9/30a.html.

Watson Institute for International Studies at Brown University. "Choices for the 21st Century." Watson Institute for International Studies at Brown University. http://www.choices.edu/.

Webster, Daniel. 1850. "The Seventh of March Speech." Dartmouth College. http://www.dartmouth.edu/~dwebster/speeches/seventh-march.html.

Weidman, Budge. "Teaching with Documents: The Fight for Equal Rights: Black Soldiers in the Civil War." U.S. National Archives and Records Administration. http://www.archives.gov/education/lessons/blacks-civil-war/article.html.

Widmer, Ted. "Old Hickory." 2005. *The Washington Post.* October 9. BW05.

Zinn, Howard. 1980. *A People's History of the United States.* New York: Harper and Row.